PRINTHOUSE BOOKS PRESENTS

I0024280

Notorious P-Man Sam
Miami's Urban Chronicles; Volume I

Thomas Barr Jr.

True Fiction

©Thomas Barr Jr.; 2015

PrintHouse Books, Atlanta, GA.

Published 4-1-2015

www.PrintHouseBooks.com

VIP INK Publishing Group; Incorporated

Thomas Barr, Jr.

Cover art, designed by SK7.
Editor: Shelby Oates

ISBN: 978-0-9861-340-1-2

Library of Congress Cataloging-in-Publication Data

1. Urban Literature 2. True Fiction
2. Business 4.Thomas Barr Jr. 5.Miami, Florida

Printed in the United States of America

I would like to acknowledge P Man Sam's

children, family and friends, Faisal X.

Tavernier for his consultation, the communities

of, Liberty City, Opa Locka, Miami (Carol City)

Gardens, North Miami, Ojus and Hialeah for

the inspiration of this novel. May this book be

a guiding light to those that seek it.

Thomas Barr, Jr.

PRINTHOUSEBOOKS.COM

This book is about the struggle of African American men as they traverse the perils of 20th and twenty first century life in the professional realms of the work place atmosphere. The differences in opportunities are often overlooked in comparison to other classes and among the races.

The American dream is the realization of success in the face of struggle and hard work. Is it relevant that one's struggle is harder than the other in accomplishment of this goal? P-Man Sam is a hard look at the road to self-empowerment and what it takes to make it in the American society. The entrepreneurial spirit is one of the main roads

traveled in realization of the American dream.

It takes knowledge and a fearlessness to take a

chance in the ruthless world of business in this

society. It's also important to be able to

effectively communicate with the modern

diverse society of today through effective

people skills.

The P-Man Sam story brings an awareness of

how to navigate negative experiences and

transform them into motivational learning

blocks. Learning from experiences and

moving forward is essential in life. One's eyes

must be open and naïve thought processes

must be conquered in attaining the ultimate

prize. The following are useful for application:

- Mentorship
- Net working
- Coalition building
- Broad-mindedness

This book is a good source for

inspiration and having hope is a major force in

your journey through life. Situations and

circumstances should not be viewed as a

hindrance, but instead a hurdle in step to the

finish line. There are many instances in this

story that relay the struggle against forces that

present obstacles. Willpower and dedication

are true factors that assist the main character in winning out against such forces.

In conclusion, the power of love and support are sustaining factors in the realization of goals in life. The act of goal-setting itself is an important factor in accomplishing anything in pursuant of ambitious dreams. This novel is sprinkled with kernels of knowledge and inspirational wording designed to give the reader insight into the motivations of the main character that can be transcending to experience.

It is beneficial and intended to identify and acquire these gems of knowledge to retain as progressive career tools.

Thomas Barr, Jr.

PRINTHOUSE BOOKS PRESENTS

ı

Notorious P-Man Sam
Miami's Urban Chronicles; Volume I

Thomas Barr Jr.

True Fiction

Table of Contents

Chapter 1: The Sequence

In the tenth year of the millennium on the major interstate of I-95 cars sped up the roadway and zinged past construction barriers. Many of the vehicles just barely swiped distressed vehicles parked roadside. Sam Silvasteen drove with his windows down taking in the South Florida breeze as his car cruised at a comfortable speed. A black car with a high performance sounding engine screeched up next to Sam's car. The sound of gunfire erupted and peppered the passenger's side with silver dollar sized bullet holes. Sam jerked the steering wheel in an attempt to dodge the spray of bullets. The men in the car continued to pace Sam's car firing ruthlessly into the frame of the automobile. Hot lead ripped through Sam's flesh as he was hit with a volley of bullets.

Sam slammed into the median and the men sped off as his car coasted to a halt along the concrete rail. Sam could hear the screaming brakes of other cars on the road and smell the scent of twisted metal as he faded out. The Entrepreneurial President of Bandstand Magazine lay shot along the Miami corridor among twisted metal. His life flashed before his eyes and he thought back on the events that led him to his current predicament.

Sam was a streetwise entrepreneur who had escaped the shadows of the crime filled eighties drug environment of Miami. Cocaine was the major drug that circulated through the community of Dade County. He transformed his life by becoming a respectable businessman and he attempted to help urban youth growing up as he did in becoming productive community citizens. Within the blink of an eye his life was turned upside down and the phantoms of his past attempted to snatch his mortal essence from existence.

Sam was initially raised in a single parent home. When Sam turned ten in the year 1977, he was placed in an orphanage by his grandparents due to his mother's early dementia among her other mental illness related problems. Sam's grandparents had six adult kids living in their home and couldn't afford a proper home for young Sam.

***

"Who turned the damn T.V.?" yelled a burly kid as his hair dripped with Jerry Curl Juice. His voice echoed through the bare white walled dayroom of the orphanage. Sam sat motionless as the other kids looked around not saying a word in response to the question. The scarcely decorated room remained silent. Most of the juveniles were Cuban exiles and spoke little English. The burly kid steaming with rage yanked the plug out of the wall and kicked the T.V. over. The loud crash and sound of breaking glass alerted the nearby sisters from the hallway entrance.

"What happened to the T.V.?" asked Sister Alice, she was new to Saint Joseph and relocated from Nicaragua to assist with the influx of prospective exiled children of political patriots. She wore the traditional long flowing robes of her profession. She was a looker and it could be speculated that she had her pick of the litter before being ordained.

"Jose kicked it over," said the burly kid as he pointed at Jose Marti, a skinny pale Cuban teen. Jose possessed long limbs, but his slender frame made him look a bit goofy in appearance.

"Jose, is this true?" replied Sister Alice, as she wheeled in his direction. Jose remained silent as Sister Alice waited for him to respond.

"Jose didn't do it Sister Alice," Sam exclaimed. His voice was firm and controlled. "Well, it didn't happen on its on Sam," replied Sister Alice in a sarcastic tone. The burly kid cut his eyes at Sam and gave him a hard look.

She now turned to the burly kid, "Trey Brownlee, if you're fibbing you get twenty lashes," she exclaimed.

"I swear....," replied Trey. Before he could finish his sentence, Sister Alice smacked him in the chest with a ruler. In a heavy Spanish accent, she sentenced Trey to spend the rest of the day in time out.

"Sam, get this mess cleaned up," she said as she escorted Trey from the room.

Sam immediately grabbed a garbage can to pick up the shards of glass that covered the floor. Jose found a broom and swept some of the glass in a pile for Sam to scoop into the garbage. The other kids resumed their activities as the hype died down.

Sam made a friend in Jose from the day of the T.V. incident with Trey. They began their friendship working as partners at anything they could do together. Sam was a husky twelve-year-old and Jose was three years his senior. The two got along quite well with no regards to their respective ages. Lucky Barnes was a younger kid who hung around Burt Ramos the only Puerto Rican kid at the orphanage. Lucky was a portly black kid with big hands. Burt often used little Lucky when he was trying to hustle the other boys in marbles.

"Hey Sam," said Burt. "Trey is going to be pissed that you stuck your nose in his business."

"Forget Trey," responded Sam. "If you're down with Trey, then forget you too," said Sam as he flopped down onto a sofa in the dayroom of the orphanage. A group of boys congregated at the corner of the day room and

shot a game of marbles.

"Oh, I'm down for myself and I was just

making sure you knew what time it was," said

Burt as he made his way to the marbles game.

Lucky gave Sam thumbs up as he shuffled

close behind Burt.

Jose pulled up a chair alongside Sam

and said, "Now we have nothing to watch

because of Trey." The boys protested loudly in

the corner of the room while Burt tried to

convince them he was not cheating. "Hey, I

got ya' back-- don't let them get to you about

that Trey stuff," he said.

Sam sat straight up and replied, "I'm not worried about a thing." He extended his hand and slapped Jose five. Jose watched a lot of T.V. and was hip to the street ways of black culture. He understood the gesture and was happy to have made a friend in a place where watching out for self was paramount. Sam was also careful in not being labeled a rat while sticking up for Jose. He knew in befriending an older kid that his chances of survival had increased tenfold.

***

The females were housed in an entirely different dorm wing as compared to the males. The only times the two would mingle were during mealtimes and that was usually three times a day. All the kids in the orphanage were supervised by nuns and the Monsignor had final call on all activities. Sam had his eye on this one pigtailed girl named Vivian Smart. She was a beautiful vivacious teen who was present at the orphanage upon Sam's arrival.

"Hi Sam," she said as she sat down with her lunch at Sam's table. "I heard what you did for that Cuban kid the other day and I think it was courageous." Sam shifted in his chair.

"No big thing," he replied. "The kid looked as if he needed help and I stepped in." Sam dropped his head and continued to munch on his sandwich. Vivian took a cookie from her tray and placed it on a napkin in front of Sam's tray. Sam didn't raise his head, but his heart quickened its pace.

"This is for your bravery," she replied as she slid the napkin in Sam's direction. Sam was at a loss for words and before he uttered his faint thank you, Vivian had strode off and rejoined her friends.

The cafeteria was a bustle with kids and they were being closely monitored by the nuns for any improprieties. Sam sat brooding as he finished his meal. He missed his mother and siblings; while the orphanage provided a vibrant surrounding, it lacked genuine personal connections. Before his mother's unfortunate problems, Sam was often doted on by his family. He was the youngest and the last born of his mother's children. His siblings were years older than he was and were all away trying to establish lives for themselves. Sam hated being poor, but what else could he do he thought to himself.

Sam made his way to the day room after lunch and sat looking out one of the windows. He had a second period of classes which he contemplated cutting. Jose walked up to him and slapped him on the back, "What up, Sam!" He said in his best English.

"What's up, Jose," replied Sam. "I got a couple of classes for second period and I do *not* feel like going," said Sam with a sigh.

Jose was only a grade higher than Sam although he was fifteen. His problems with the language barrier relegated him to grades lower than his normal level in Cuba. "Let's hang out in the courtyard or sneak over to the girl's dorm," replied Jose.

"Cool," replied Sam. He stashed his books under a nearby sofa and was out the door along with Jose.

***

The girl's wing was well kept and immaculate in comparison to the facilities the

26

boys maintained. When not in class, the girls milled around outside and played dodge ball on the cement courts. The males and females rarely participated in physical activities together except when there was a yearly festival occurring. Jose and Sam hid behind a dumpster near the courts of the girl's dormitory. "Hey, there's Vivian," said Sam as he ducked so he wouldn't be seen by her.

"Who is Vivian?" Jose inquired.

"Nobody," replied Sam.

The girls walked on a nearby court and began their ritual jump rope Double Dutch game. Jose whistled trying to get one of the girl's attention, Sam nudged him in the side.

27

"Are you trying to get us busted?" exclaimed Sam.

"No, just trying to get us some trim," replied Jose.

One of the girls heard the commotion and walked over to where Sam and Jose were held up. She saw them crouched behind the dumpster and immediately began screaming. The boys tore out of their hiding place and ran for the nearest place to duck for cover. Jose laughed hysterically as he tried to catch his breath from the sprint to the dormitory.

"You're crazy," remarked Sam bending over in exhaustion.

"That was a rush," said Jose.

***

The two boys walked back to the dayroom and talked about the look on the girls' faces when they realized they were being spied upon. Classes were ending for the day and the dayroom was filled with students. Music appreciation seminars were usually held by Sister Alice after dinner and Sam really enjoyed the sessions. He profiled the different types of music genres as well as the musicians of past and contemporary times. "I'm going to my room before dinner," said Jose.

"See you later," remarked Sam.

Sam remained in the dayroom leafing through his school books as he sat on a bench in the back of the room. Sister Alice entered the dayroom recruiting groups to complete chores. Sister Alice mentioned that the females were also participating and Sam decided to volunteer. One group of males and one group of females were directed to the gymnasium area of the compound. The two groups were instructed to scrub the floors and wash the walls. Sam joined the chore group hoping to get a chance to be around Vivian. Sam began scrubbing and to his dismay saw no sign of Vivian in the other group.

Sam continued to volunteer his services for Sister Alice's chore squad in hopes of seeing Vivian. On this one particular day the squad was tasked to clean the main administrative offices of parish officials.

Vivian was assigned to the task and Sam was delighted his persistence had finally paid off. Sam decided he would work closely with Vivian and learn more about her interests.

"Hey, what are you doing here?" said Sam. Vivian stopped what she was doing and put her hands on her hips.

"The same thing you're doing," she said. The girls giggled as Vivian smiled at Sam.

Sam thought to himself that was a dumb question to ask. He never knew the right words to say to the members of the opposite sex. She looked so beautiful standing there with a twinkle in her eyes and sass in her voice thought Sam.

"Well, I was offering to help, but I see you're good," Sam replied with a smirk.

"You're such a good guy," said Vivian with a wink.

Sam continued to work while the girls chatted about what guys they thought were cute in the boys' dormitory. Sam pondered his next move on how to get Vivian's attention without her friends being around. He thought he would have a better chance at an honest conversation on a one-on-one basis. Sam would have to covertly recruit individuals to help with his plan and a major part of his plan would be Sister Alice.

Sam was exhausted after his chores so he lounged in the dayroom and watched the boys roll marbles. A couple of maintenance men coordinated the installment of a new T.V. in place of the damaged one. Jose walked in and made his way over to a nearby sofa avoiding the guys on the floor as they shot marbles.

"So, you were doing chores," remarked Jose. "Did you see your sweetheart, Vivian?" He uttered with a laugh. Sam ignored Jose's commentary and continued to watch the boys argue over taking a turn to roll marbles.

"When are you going to volunteer to help out around here?" asked Sam. "Maybe you'll meet a nice female." Sam remarked.

"My uncles say the best way to get a fine girl is with a lot of money," said Jose.

"Yeah, that works too," said Sam with a chuckle.

Sam was intent on winning the heart of Vivian and he assured himself that love was his reason for his persistence. Sam had not really known the love of a woman outside of his mother, but he could not resist the emotion he felt when he was around Vivian. Sam was careful about revealing his feelings around the people he interacted with daily though because in his environment this could be a source of perceived weakness.

Trey entered the dayroom and stomped through the circled marbles on the floor where the boys were shooting them. The sound of grinding glass against the floor could be heard as Trey twisted his foot on each stomp. Marbles shot out from under Trey's foot hitting the sides of nearby chairs, tables and walls. The boys scuttled out of Trey's path dodging the flying marbles as they moved out of the way.

"Man, why'd you do that?!" One of the enraged boys responded.

"Shut your trap," retorted Trey.

Sam knew Trey was pissed he had challenged his rule in standing up for Jose. Sam was ready for whatever retaliation Trey would seek to impose. Sam continued to lounge nonchalantly on the sofa as Trey marauded around the dayroom. Jose remained silent as he sat on the other sofa. Sam could see Jose was tense and his demeanor had drastically shifted in relation to his earlier mood. Sister Alice stuck her head through the doorway of the day room.

"We will have no trouble out of you today, Trey," she said as she disappeared down the hallway.

Sam sat at the breakfast table alone and ate his bowl of oatmeal in silence. He soon felt a hand on his shoulder. It was Sister Alice standing over him smiling with her black nun's veil draped over her hair.

"Sam, don't mind Trey much," she said. "Both his parents died of AIDS when he was just a toddler." She pulled up a chair and sat next to Sam. Sam paused between spoons full of oatmeal as she continued to talk.

"He was raised by his grandmother until she died a couple of months ago and he seems to have a hard time adjusting." She said.

Sam thought to himself he was not having an easy time here either and why is she telling this story to someone who loathes Trey. Sam began to fidget with his silverware as Sister Alice told Trey's life story. He desperately wished Jose would appear and interrupt her oration. Sam could appreciate the concern Sister Alice felt for the kids of the orphanage. He wondered if she spoke of his situation and issues with others as she did of Trey.

Sam's own home situation was what led to his current occupancy and he felt little empathy for Trey's story. Sam had few adult role models; however, Sister Alice influenced the good in him. Sam dreamed of the day when he could stand on his own without the need of the orphanage. He was tired of being a kid and was ready to venture out into the world. Sam was in his own thoughts now and subconsciously caught bits and pieces of Sister Alice's conversation. "You know, Sam, Saint Joseph will seek to be a solid base for your upbringing as you grow up," she said. Her voice seemed to trail off as her last comment reverberated in his thoughts.

Sam desired to make a good impression on others by making himself who they thought he should be. He would do tasks that made other people happy and would go all out to fit in with others. Sam felt uneasy in the aftermath when he thought of this act of self repression. His true nature was to be himself and explore who the real Sam was as an individual.

Sam viewed Trey as a bully and an enemy to the free spirit of those around him. Trey's bully tactics blunted the freewill of others stunting their growth. Sam in an attempt to be ordinary like everyone else downplayed his true abilities. He had no desire to be recognized as exceptional in comparison to his colleagues. The Trey-types sought to bring out such exceptional abilities which made Sam hate him even more.

Sam's perceived abandonment issues stoked his desires for the camaraderie of others and he highly valued friendship. Trey's bullying tampered with that concept which in turn was a source for instability in Sam's world. Sam would mesh out any instability that threatened his contentment. Trey would be met with the harsh retaliation whenever he threatened to disrupt Sam's reality.

Sister Alice realized Sam was not soaking in her words and stopped speaking. She looked at Sam as he sat gazing into the distance. She raised herself from her seated position and stood with her hands on her hips.

She shook her head and walked away from

Sam as he continued his gaze.

"Kids," she said.

Chapter 2: The Block

Sam spent eighteen years of his teen life growing up in an orphanage. At nineteen he was now a young man on a mission. It was now 1981 and Sam had an apartment in the heart of Miami's Liberty City neighborhood. It had all the accompaniments of modern living and was not like the dingy suites of his neighbors. He worked at a nearby Burger King as a cook and had married his childhood sweet heart, Vivian.

Sam was ambitious and worked long hours to provide the better things in life for his lovely bride. Sam stood on the front porch of his apartment and enjoyed a smoke off his Black & Mild Cigar. He wasn't due at work until 2pm and he wanted to relax a bit before going in. It was noon and the street was active with people walking to and fro. Sam flicked the butt of his cigar to the porch floor and decided to go in to work early. He skipped off the porch and walked two blocks before he viewed a candy apple painted Mercedes Benz on the corner.

Standing outside of the car smoking a joint was a tall skinny Cuban male. His hair was jet black and slicked back dangled with curls. He wore a grey silk suit with gold rings on each of his pinky fingers. He leaned leisurely against the Benz and the sunglasses he wore glittered like a camera lens.

"I heard you lived around here," he commented. "Heading to your job at Burger King," he asked as he removed his sunglasses.

Before Sam was cognizant of it he blurted out, "Jose Marti!" The two young men grasped the other's hand shaking it while they gave each other a half embrace. "Man, you look like you just stepped off the front cover of GQ," remarked Sam.

"You can look this way to my brother," said Jose. His English had greatly improved, but he still maintained a heavy accent.

The two young men strolled up the street in conversation as they dodged oncoming pedestrians walking the opposite direction.

"How did you find me?" inquired Sam.

"I kept in touch with Sister Alice over the years," said Jose. "She told me you lived in this area," he commented. "I also heard you finally locked down your girl," said Jose with a wry smile.

Sam chuckled, "Yeah, something like that."

Jose smiled. "Well, congratulations, you deserve to be happy," he commented as his voice trailed off in a whisper.

"What's going on with you man?" asked Sam with a curious look of concern on his face.

"Listen," said Jose. He now spoke slowly and deliberately. "You always had my back when we were younger and I never forgot that." Jose whirled to face Sam eye-to-eye. "I need you to have my back again." Sam struggled to grasp the meaning of what Jose was trying to say. "I now work for my father's baby brother and I get a lot of static from folks," said Jose. "I need someone at my back that I can trust and it's you," stated Jose. Sam immediately started nodding his head no.

"Man, I have a family now and I am trouble free," Sam stated. A car blew its horn in the street as they carried on their discussion. "I have a chance to do things the right way and besides, I got a job," he stated.

"I hear you working man," Jose replied with a smirk. He placed his polished lens sunglasses back on his olive complexion face and brushed the front of his suit with his hands.

"You need a ride to work," asked Jose.

Sam replied, "No, we're here."

Jose was unaware they had covered two blocks while they chatted and had reached BK while his car sat parked on the street.

"Damn, you're right," he replied. "I'll be around," Jose said. He gave Sam a pound and smiled.

Sam replied, "Yeah," with a laugh and dabbed him back.

Sam entered his work place with a lot on his mind. He had seen an old friend that he had not heard from since childhood. His friend now appeared to be very successful and sought to share the wealth. Sam experienced the despair of loneliness and abject poverty as a young child. He desired more for his own family and didn't want to be just another flash in the pan. Sam thought back to his mother and his own experience with her attempting to raise him. He had vowed to himself that family was more than anything and it was his personal vow to keep above all things.

Jose had a similar life experience to his own with a twist, however. He was an immigrant and his motivations were a more ferocious pursuit of the American dream. He had experienced utter poverty and a dysfunctional family upbringing. He found a kindred spirit with Sam and they soldiered on confronting the perils of society. Sam pondered if he had insulted Jose in not accepting his offer. It was Jose's honest attempt at reaching out to help a friend who did the same years ago. The pair was now grown and the loyalty back then had since shifted in its priority. Sam hated being put in this type of position and regretted the whole encounter with Jose. Yet, the situation had occurred and that's the way the ball bounces. Sam had no intention on compromising his beliefs for the sake of Jose. He would have to solve his dilemma with the least drama as possible.

***

A couple of weeks had passed since Sam's encounter with Jose and he wondered what had become of his friend. It was a Saturday and he was not scheduled to work for the entire day. As he sat in his tiny apartment he pondered what to do of his day of work and smartly decided to go up the block to the pool hall.

He skipped down his front steps and walked leisurely with his hands in his pockets toward the direction of the pool hall. The sun was blazing with people walking about and children playing in the street. As Sam neared the pool hall he noticed a black Porsche parked along the street. He stopped and admired the nice tires on the car before entering the establishment. Sam thought of owning such a car and he was tired of not having his own transportation. He had gotten his license on his last birthday and was unable to save for a car due to mounting bills at home. As he turned from admiring the car to go into the establishment he bumped into a group of guys as they were coming out.

"Watch it, slick, you almost stepped on a pair of hundred dollar sneakers," said a guy in the party. Sam adjusted his step and kept walking.

"Did you hear what he said, cupcake?" asked another guy in the crew.

Sam spun around with his back facing the door and was about four feet from the last of the three guys. They all wore silk T-shirts with Levi Jeans and the last guy that spoke stood with his hand to his side slightly behind his right leg. Before Sam could say a word he heard a voice from behind him.

"Whoa fellas, you don't want none of this man he's a beast!" it bellowed.

Sam knew the voice as it began to laugh and he felt a slap on his back. It was Jose. Sam noticed the last guy slowly slip something in the small of his back before revealing his now visible hand. The other two guys relaxed and the tension dissipated between the four on the street.

"Man, what you doin' here?" asked Jose.

"Just hangin'," replied Sam still salty from his encounter with Jose's crew.

"I'm glad I ran into you," said Jose. "I might have some part time work for you. I know you need the money," he said. "I'm starting my own DJ music group and I need you." He unclipped a pager from his belt and handed it to Sam. "Take this; I'll hit you with the details." Jose turned and jumped in the Porsche with his crew. As the car spun out with a loud screech he could hear Jose's voice once again. "See you soon," he said as his voice trailed off.

Sam knew that DJ's in the city were very competitive. Miami DJ's battled for the limelight of having the best system and loudest quality sound. The unique DJing technique of regulating a record was very popular in the city. DJ's would cut the record down to change the lyrics of the song, then say something and have the record answer back. The crowd loved the call and response DJing at house parties.

Sam had maintained relations with Burt Ramos from the days of being in the orphanage and often saw him in the neighborhood. As

Sam stood in front of the pool hall Burt walked up from a back alley.

"Man, that was a sweet all black Porsche," he remarked. Sam was jarred from his inner thoughts.

"Remember Jose Marti from St. Joseph?" he inquired.

"Yeah, what about him?" remarked Burt.

"That was him," said Sam. He pulled the door to the pool hall open and entered. Burt followed him in and questioned him.

"What's up with him, Sam?" he asked.

Sam slid into an open booth by the door of the pool hall and Burt sat across from him on the opposite side.

"He's going into the music businesses and is forming a DJ group," said Sam, "He wants me to run it."

"Well, you know Trey Brownlee has the group Double M DJ's," replied Burt.

The music in the pool hall was loud and the clacking of balls could be heard throughout the building. Sam sat with his hands clasped on top of the table and Burt leaned in over the table in discussion.

"That kid makes 10 tapes a day: specialty tapes, custom-made tapes, and regular mixes, selling them for $10 to $35 dollars each," said Burt. "$500 in Ft. Lauderdale and $1000 every other week in Miami," he said. Sam listened with interest as he had no idea such a thriving market existed in this underground movement. "Imagine if you were making that kind of money with Jose backing you," said Burt. He leaned back in his seat confident that he got his point across.

"Whatcha' having?" inquired the waitress as she tapped a pencil on a semi rolled up pad she held.

"Two beers and some wings," shot Burt. "This is on him," he gestured toward Sam while rubbing his palms together.

Jose already had a crew, Sam thought to himself. Why would he want to bring someone in from the outside on that type of score? Sam decided for that type of money it was worth seeing it thru. He appreciated Burt sharing that bit of news with him; he decided to purchase another round of beers. It was a good feeling to have opportunities in life, he thought as he motioned for the waitress.

Sam's desire to make money was fueled by his fear of not being able to provide for his loved ones. In addition to not wanting to be poor, he wanted to make the lives of those he loved bearable. He often questioned his morality of associating himself with those individuals he deemed as criminal in nature. Is it wrong to break societal rules in attempting to better your lot without causing harm to others? He would often ask himself this provocative question. Sam believed in the rule of law. But what if the rule of law was stifling one group while serving as a benefit for another group or groups. In American society the lady of justice wears a blindfold as she balances the scale. This is an example of symbolism and its unspoken words are universally understood as fairness. What if this is not the case for his kind? He would sometimes ask in his many self reflections.

However, Sam knew that in order to function in this society one had to play by the rules. The game of life was meant to be played with the awareness of who calls the shots and when to fold if required. As long as he could see that things were on the up-and-up he would take Burt's advice on this money making venture.

The reason for Burt pushing the issue was because he wanted to get in on the action. He knew that Sam would cut him in on the venture and quite possibly drop the entire day-to-day running of the operation in his lap. He knew Sam was savvy when it came to street life, but his desire was that of business. Burt was a party person and wanted to be flashy for the women he lusted after on the streets. This presented two distinct perspectives and the two considered the venture.

Chapter 3: The Players

Sam was experiencing severe cuts in his hours at work and desperately needed another income stream. He sat home one Thursday night, his off day and fingered the pager given to him earlier by Jose. He wondered how many hands the pager had gone through before reaching his. It felt like a wad of money as it poked out of his pocket. This is how it must feel to have a knot thought Sam to himself. The pager started to vibrate nonstop to his surprise and he jumped to his feet in amazement. He looked around the apartment for a phone by reflex. He paused and thought to himself it would be better to use a pay phone to return the call. "Going up the block, I'll be back in a minute," he said aloud before bounding out the door.

***

The street was busy with people and Sam made his way over to the pool hall located on 62nd street. The pager continued to go off and Sam dialed up the incoming number on the nearest phone he found. "What's up, bro!" said the voice on the receiver. "Where are you?" Sam could tell that the voice was Jose's and he relayed his location as that of the pool hall. "I'll be over to pick you up," said Jose before he ended the call. A half hour passed and Jose pulled up in an all red Ferrari with black leather interior.

"What's up Sam, hop in," he said.

"Where we headed," Sam replied as he lowered the suicide doors of the Ferrari.

The car screeched off from the curb and it seemed to glide over the road as Jose shifted through the gears. The inside of the car was all leather with chrome instrument gauges and digital display panels. Sam ran his fingers across the leather dash and was amazed how smooth the texture of the surface was. It was hard for him to imagine the life style that his friend Jose was living. They both had met at the same juncture in their lives and taken different paths. His led to marriage and a steady job to pay the bills. Jose's branched into the flamboyant lifestyle of glitzy cars and tough guy personas. Sam was dumbfounded at how life's path unfolds.

"Here's the deal" said Jose. "As my partner I want you to help me with this music business that I'm trying to establish."

Sam thought about the viability of a business in music and was concerned with the stability of the idea. His hours were getting shorter at work and he knew this opportunity with Jose could make up the difference.

"Sure, I'm in," said Sam.

"Cool," replied Jose. "We're back together again bro."

***

Sam stood on his apartment veranda and pondered working with his old friend Jose. It would be fun, he thought to himself. Just like the old days back, when they were young, he reminisced. The street was abuzz with people as it was usually. A few individuals shot salutations to Sam as they passed on the street. Sam knew that he would need to devote time to his business venture with Jose. He still needed to work his job until it was feasible to quit.

Sam's wife Vivian worked as a beautician at a neighborhood salon and was not due home until late. Sam locked the front door of his apartment and stepped off onto the street. He walked a block and turned onto

Sistrunk Street. There was an all-white Cadillac convertible parked on the curb with the top down. In the car sat the reputed king of MIA, Bo Diddley. He puffed on a Cuban cigar as Sam passed him and his crew on the street.

"Yo, man," said a voice.

Sam turned to see who had spoken and realized it was Diddley. He raised himself halfway out the car with one hand on the driver's side door window. His neck glimmered in the sunlight from the many gold herringbone chains he wore.

"Ain't you Jose's home boy?" he inquired as smoke bellowed out the corners of his well-manicured, bearded mouth.

"Yeah," replied Sam.

"I heard a lot about you my nigga'," he said, "Jose my home boy."

Sam nodded.

"Holla' at me if you need something," he said as he slid back into his white leather crush seats.

Sam continued on his way speculating what that exchange actually meant. Bo had risen from a working man to the king of dope in the Miami street life. He didn't know that Jose had contacts with such a person. Diddley was a real heavy weight and his impressions of Jose were from youth orphanage days. Sam could hardly believe that Sam, an immigrant from Cuba, had dealings with the neighborhood kingpin.

Sam peered across the street and could see two people stacking four-foot tall base bin speakers one atop another. He recognized Burt Ramos as one of the individuals and he crossed the street to see what was happening.

"What up, Sam," said Burt, as he struggled to stack a speaker on one that was sitting on the curb. "Lucky and I started our own crew," he said with a smile, Ghetto Style DJ's. Lucky struggled with a speaker bin and slammed it on the pavement.

"It's been a while, Sam," he said, as he wiped sweat from his brow.

"Yeah," replied Sam, "too long."

Burt and Lucky had been friends just as Sam and Jose had been during their time at the orphanage.

"So, you thought about it and was motivated by your own idea," said Sam to Burt with a smirk on his face.

"Hey, there's enough for everyone to go around," replied Burt with a chuckle.

Sam realized that Burt had extensive first-hand knowledge on the burgeoning underground DJ music scene. He wondered if Jose was as knowledgeable as Burt or was he just in it to build upon his reputation in the community. Burt cranked on an electric generator, soon his system was on and blasting. The music was so loud it seemed to vibrate for blocks as people gathered and tapped their feet to the bass.

***

Jose owned a storage warehouse on the far side of town and Sam arrived there with the intension of talking business with him. The warehouse was located in a deserted industrial business district in the seedy part of the city. Sam tapped on the aluminum door and it jerked open abruptly to his surprise. A muscled figured black guy stood in the doorway. Sam was familiar with the guy from the neighborhood.

"What's up, Heavy Face," said Sam, "Jose around?"

"Come on in Sam," replied Heavy Face as he slapped Sam on the back. "He's waiting inside for you."

Sam had always wondered how'd the name Heavy Face was earned as a nickname and was silently amused whenever he heard it. Sam had considered the name of the group after hearing Burt and Lucky's group name. He liked the name Space Funk DJ's and would pose it to Jose.

The warehouse was spacious with a closed booth office located in the far rear of the building. It sat in the industrial zoned part of the city and had sparse foot traffic along the streets. Crated boxes covered the middle floor section of the warehouse and factory machinery lined the walls. Sam was led to the office and was greeted by Jose at the door.

"You found the place, huh," he jested.

Sam peered around the office, found the nearest chair and sat down. He could smell the scent of motor oil and sea water in the air. He felt exhausted from his sojourn to meet with Jose regarding the business venture.

"The group's name will be Space Funk DJ's and we will need the best equipment to compete out in these streets," said Sam sternly.

"I like that," replied Jose, "Sounds like you've given this venture serious thought."

Jose sat across the room and kicked his feet up on his desk while reclining in his gator skinned chair. His office was sparsely decorated and Sam could tell that he spent little time at the location and wondered why they met there in the first place.

"I'll get the truck and the audio equipment this weekend," he said.

There was a loud clang out on the floor of the warehouse. Heavy Face along with a couple of other workers dropped a crate they were loading onto a pallet. The commotion from outside the office was loud drawing Sam's attention. He walked over to the doorway and peered out to see what was going on.

"Those guys out there will be your crew," said Jose.

Sam desired to have his own handpicked guys with whom to work. He valued loyalty among all things in associations. But he would work with Jose and see how things would go.

***

Chapter 4:

Music Entertainment Industry

The streets of Liberty City Miami were like any in a predominantly black lower-middle class area. Crack cocaine was introduced; gangs and crews fought for territory and this new hip-hop phenomenon filled the South Florida air. Local DJ's in South Florida's music culture moved the crowd with two turntables and a microphone. DJ's battled each other in parks, in the streets, and on the block. The bass music break beats of Afro-Rican, Beat Master Clay D and Jiggalo Tony were a rumble in the streets.

Sam formulated the idea of selling the crew's taped music sessions at the local flea markets of 183rd and USA One. The money flowed and Sam soon quit his job at the fast food joint to focus solely on the music business. Just as Burt had said the tapes were generating a profit of five hundred dollars a week.

Just as the music entertainment business was experiencing success, unbeknownst to Sam so was Jose's other underground business activities. Jose was affiliated with the Cocaine Cowboy movement and was making money hand over fist. With the proceeds from his drug movement, he funneled it into his music entertainment business. Jose put money into purchasing a moving truck to haul around all equipment needed for the business. He also put money into buying generators and electrical equipment to have self-sustained power for music events. Audio equipment such as: microphones, mixers, turntables, bass bins, speakers, amplifiers and equalizers were purchased.

Although the music entertainment business was a success, the crew faced a problem with the crew of Trey Brownlee and the Double M DJ's. Trey's Crew would usually set up on 54th Street in the city. They assembled their speakers and audio equipment to blast the music and jam for the local crowds. The tension started when the Double M DJ's felt that the Space Funk DJ's were encroaching on their turf.

Sam, Heavy Face and the rest of the Space Funk DJ crew began unloading speakers and equipment from the box truck. They had decided to set up on 62nd Street for an afternoon of funk and party music. All the guys were on the back of the truck struggling with a four-foot base bin speaker. Sam was up front standing on the street with his back turned towards the roadway. He soon felt what he assumed was a nozzle pressed up against his side.

"What up, fuck nigga'," said a voice from his rear, instantly he recognized the voice as Trey Brownlee.

Sam stiffened and took a deep breath,

"Trey, it's Sam," he said.

"I know who it is," remarked Trey.

He removed the nozzle from Sam's side

as he took a step back. Sam slowly turned

around and recognized the weapon as an AK-

47 assault rifle, known in the streets as a

chopper. Trey folded the stock on the weapon

and slipped it into a knapsack. He then slung

it onto his back.

"I heard yawl boys had a crew, I had to

see it with my own eyes," said Trey. He was

dressed in a short sleeved all-black Dickies

work set.

Sam inched close to Trey and whispered, "This isn't St. Joseph, and if I ever see that gun again I'll bury you."

Heavy Face emerged from the rear, "Problem here? ---Problem, nigga'," he again repeated his inquiry directed at Trey.

With his hands raised, he backed away slowly. He commented, "No problem."

Sam assumed Trey was curious about the competition and decided to do some premature scouting on his own. Word of mouth of the Space Funk DJ's was positive in the hood.

***

Heavy Face relayed the run in Sam had with Trey and Jose's reaction was surprising to say the least. Instead of reacting violently, Jose was remarkably calm; he seemed as if it was a planned meet. Sam knew that he would eventually have to meet face-to-face with Trey and would next time be ready for him.

Jose, as a budding member of the Cocaine Cowboys, was making a name for himself in the streets of Miami. Jose hooked up with a gang of Colombians and drug smuggling became the business of South Florida. Jose's knowledge of the Hispanic neighborhood and access to the black community made him invaluable to the Colombians. He was more a distributer for their product instead of a seller.

The Colombians used freighter ships to smuggle pounds of cocaine thru the port of Miami. Jose's crew downloaded the dope and divvied it out to the peddlers in the local communal areas of the city. Often times shipments of 35 pounds of product were obtained by Jose for wholesale. Sixteen thousand bricks from a 35 pound shipment were worth millions of dollars in the hood.

Sam was street savvy and knowledgeable of the code of the hustlers in the city's neighborhoods. He decided to check in with Burt and gleam any information regarding Trey's movements in the street. Burt resided in a warehouse apartment and as Sam entered he spied Lucky sitting at a fold-up card table.

"What up, Sam," said Lucky, "What you know 'bout this?"

Lucky had a half-ounce bag of cocaine he had cooked down and he sifted two grams of baking powder into the stash. He then boiled it in a beaker with water. It formed a solid mass and took the form of what looked like a cookie. He placed it on a paper towel and it cooled. After it cooled he cut it into pieces and bagged it in little plastic bags.

"I didn't know this was a crack house," said Sam as he placed his hand over his mouth to hold back a half laugh.

"Fuck you, nigga'," replied Lucky, "I'm gonna' get mines."

Burt soon emerged from a door in the rear of the residence.

"What up, playboy," he said, "heard you finally met up with Trey."

"Yeah, it wasn't anything to it," replied Sam.

"You know he's pissed you guys are moving in on his turf," said Burt.

"He has been making money from his spot for a long time and he feels threatened."

Sam remarked with a soft giggle, "He should because we got that funk for the people."

"Naw, we got the funk," replied Burt, "Right Lucky?"

Lucky looked up from the card table and gave a quick nod. He continued to concentrate on bagging the product. Sam did not know that Burt and Lucky were active in the drug game here in the city. He himself tried to steer clear of that life; however, he was never the one to knock another man's hustle. In the neighborhood, slinging dope was equivalent to playing sports, the dozens or racing. Acclaim and acknowledgement were heaped on those that excelled at being the best. Living in the hood was competitive and as a young man in the city of Miami it was a way of life. When one is considered the best, he or she has access to avenues that the average person is not privy to experience. Friends come more easily, money comes easy and females are a lot friendlier when you're recognized as the best. At this point in time in the city, outside of schooling, the avenues to success were drugs, music and pimping. Sam was making good money in the DJ entertainment business and making a solid reputation in the community. He would venture out more as a businessman and persuade Jose to go into the gentlemen's club business.

***

Chapter 5: Strip Clubs

Gentlemen's cabarets in Miami were a big thing among the area bikers and DJ's made big money spinning records for the dancers. The strip club venue was a great way to break new music and Sam decided to persuade Jose to start a new business. They could get their music regular play for a fixed audience and have it adopted industry-wide for regular play. Sam approached Jose with the idea and Club Polo's was formed.

***

Jose was initially skeptical about the idea of a strip club. He believed it was more work than it was worth. Strippers were essentially independent contractors. The dancers sign a contract to work in the club, but are not employees. They agree to work at least three six-hour shifts a week, but come in whenever they wish. There is no set schedule and a list of "on-call girls" is kept, if enough dancers don't show.

The dancers pay to work. The females pay the house according to the time they arrive: $10 at noon, $20 from noon to 7 p.m., $30 after 7 p.m. and $50 starting at midnight. If they show up early, they can pay at the end of their shift. If they show up at midnight, they have to pay up front. Most clubs charge girls $7 per stage dance and other fees to work the private VIP rooms, all of which is tracked through standard bookkeeping measures. The dancers who work more than five days in a single week get the sixth and seventh days at no cost. Girls that make more than $500 for the house in a week become a member of the "500 Club." That means they can work as little as they'd like the next week.

Strip clubs also like cabbies. Most clubs give taxi and limo drivers $5 a head for every customer they bring to the club. These so-called "cab redemption fees" are payable on the spot and can increase, if the driver keeps a steady stream coming. So, if you see a stretch limo parked out front, chances are the driver is having a good night.

No change necessary. Out of singles to tip the dancers? Not to worry. The club has you covered. Most clubs keeps a large stash of $1 bills on hand to maximize the customer experience. It's not unheard of for a customer to ask for $500 in ones and the club is happy to oblige. Guys can charge the festivities to their credit cards and get redeemable "funny money" for tipping the dancers and managers.

Being a manager takes good people skills. Running a strip club, more than anything, requires patience and solid listening skills. The job is comparable to babysitting. The drama is usually with the girls and intoxicated customers that come from other clubs. The real laborious work is keeping dancers on the floor and managing their problems outside the club, from boyfriend fights to money issues. When business is slow, the dancers likely tend to hang out in the dressing room and gossip, often resulting in arguments.

A sale is a sale. Occasionally managers get grief from customers, mainly in the form of "Monday morning buyer's remorse." They call the club saying they never intended to spend $1,200 over the weekend. Research is often required when going into business for oneself.

***

It was opening night and the staff of the club was readying the club for its public debut. As part owner, Sam handled marketing and direct supervision of employees was left to the manager hired by Jose.

"Are you going to stick around later for the club opening?" Sam asked Jose as they sat at the bar.

"I have something to take care of and I will probably be back later," Jose replied.

"You know that thing with Trey, it's really an irritation," said Jose.

"Don't worry, partner," Sam quipped, "that fool's all mouth."

Jose knocked back a shot glass full of cognac and slammed it to the bar as he frowned from the strong after taste of the liquor. Sam knew Jose was contemplating on what to do concerning the Brownlee situation and was guarded on his responses.

"I'll check in later," said Jose as he walked away from the bar.

The bartender removed Jose's shot glass. "Anything else, boss?" he inquired of Sam.

"I'm good," Sam responded.

It was around midnight when the club came to life with women bare chested and bouncing their big booty bottoms on the laps of paying customers. Heavy Face was the appointed DJ for the night and he played music requested by the dancers for their customers. The club's ambiance was beach party inspired. Bamboo tables and coconut trees were set throughout the floor. Drinks were served in miniature cup barrels while guys with fists of dollar bills made it rain on the succulent dancers.

Sam worked the crowd and made sure to take care of all the patrons. He noticed many guys he knew from the neighborhood. He soon viewed Jose as he entered with an entourage of people headed towards VIP. VIP was specialized accommodations for the big spenders and was cordoned off from regular seating. Sam wondered if Jose had a planned run in with Trey. He could see that Jose was troubled before he departed the club earlier. He decided to have a chat with him when the opportunity presented itself.

Sam and Jose made thousands of dollars within a couple of months from their DJ hustle on the streets. They made thousands of dollars in their strip club in one night in their new role as legitimate businessmen. The club turned out to be a success and the following afternoon Sam sat with Jose to complete the financial audit.

"I saw you with your entourage, how did things go?" asked Sam.

"Fine, got a lot done," said Jose.

Jose appeared to have a hangover. He sipped on a glass of lemon water and knocked back a couple of aspirins. Sam thought Jose's response peculiar and he continued to chip at Jose with questions.

"What did you think of last night?" He asked.

"We made money, it was fabulous," replied Jose.

Jose took another sip from his glass of water and started to pace the floor. He seemed pensive and agitated.

"You don't have to worry about any problems with Trey," he said. "My guys handled that issue."

"What happened," Sam replied. Jose had his full attention now.

"We caught him up at the pack jam in a back alley with a chick," said Jose. "We took the back exit to avoid the crowd when we left the club; he was making out with the girl."

Sam dropped his gaze to the floor and began nodding his head. He could not believe what he was hearing. Trey was an asshole since childhood, but this was definitely an unfortunate thing.

"We snatched him up and stomped out his kneecaps," said Jose, "he was wallowing around in that alley, kneecaps all busted crying like a bitch." His accent was strong and the way he pronounced the words he spoke almost made Sam laugh. I guess Trey had been asking for that beat down for years thought Sam to himself. Size really doesn't matter in this time and age when it can be equalized with a crew of bruisers.

***

Chapter 6: The Demise

Sam's entrepreneurial spirit was ignited by the business tentacles of the music entertainment business. He thought the heavy handed techniques of Jose could be a bad thing for business. He fully expected retaliation from Trey's camp and was unsure how it would be manifested. He brooded over the dilemma while he sipped a cup of coffee in the kitchen of his apartment. Vivian entered the kitchen; she moved about as pots rattled on the stove. She then dropped a plate and it smashed to the floor with a loud crash. Sam sensed that something was eating at her and could feel a flash of hotness shoot through his body.

"What's the problem?" He snapped as he turned to face her while seated in his chair.

"I'm tired of the late hours you keep," she replied. "I'm always eating dinner alone or with my girls, on account you're always out."

Steam rose from Sam's coffee cup and he blew slightly over the hot liquid as he continued to sip. He worried that this very instant could happen and was surprised Vivian had not made a fuss sooner. The money he was making was good, much better than working those low wage fast food jobs. He had found a legitimate hustle and was going to ride the wave until it went bust.

"Aren't the bills being paid around here," stated Sam with irritation in his voice.

He dug into his pocket and pulled out a wad of rolled up dollar bills in a rubber band. He placed the money on the corner of the table.

"This is what late nights get you," he said.

Vivian stepped over the shards of dismembered plate on the floor, snatched the money from the table and walked out of the room. Sam was left in peace and continued to sip idly on his coffee.

***

Sam entered the barbershop on 62nd Avenue in Liberty City, All City Cuts. He decided to get his head shaved today and have his goatee lined up. Jose often got his hair cut in the shop as well and he hoped to bump into him today. He greeted the guys in the shop before he sat down in the barber's chair for his cut.

"Anybody seen Jose?" He asked.

One of the barbers pointed to the door as Jose was walking up to enter the shop. He was alone which Sam found unusual as he often traveled with an entourage of people.

"What up, homeboy," he said to Sam as he slapped him five.

Jose sat in a barber's chair near the door and chatted about some new girls he had auditioned for work at the club.

"Homeboy, I got two stallions from Atlanta that's gonna' start in the club," he said.

Sam listened as the barber ran the clippers over his head and the hair dropped into his face. He squirmed in his chair to remove the itchy follicles from his nose and continued to listen to Jose talk about the women.

Sam had a busy day ahead of him and when he was done left the shop. Before leaving he assured Jose they would meet up at the club later to get the girls situated with work schedules at the club. Sam continued to make good money with the Space Funk DJ music group and toyed with the idea of letting the strip club business go. It was causing stress in his marriage and he had worked hard at his relationship with Vivian. However, the money was good and Sam knew what it was like to be broke with no income stream.

Sam was curious about what rumors were rampant on the streets and decided to head over to Burt's place for a visit. Burt was always up on street gossip and knew people that knew people. They perpetually kept him in the loop of what was occurring on the streets and he would relay that information to his associates.

Just as Sam met up with Burt on the block setting up his DJ equipment, he noticed he looked a bit shaken.

"Everything good with you man?" asked Sam.

"Man, they got your boy," Burt replied shaking his head from side to side.

"What are you talking about?!" exclaimed Sam. He had a bad feeling the entire day and Burt had just verified it at this moment.

"He was at the barbershop and they shot him," said Burt. Jose was shot and his uncle is dead.

"I just left the shop," said Sam as his voice trailed off into a whisper.

"He was getting shaved with a straight razor with his chair back and a towel over his face like how the old gangsters do it," said

105

Burt, "when two armed gunmen ran in the shop and shot him in the head." Burt placed a hand on Sam's shoulder.

"He never saw it coming," said Burt.

Sam was in disbelief of the news and did not want to show too much emotion in the presence of Burt. Jose had been a friend from his childhood and the years they knew each other were comparable to that of family. The streets could be brutal and Sam felt a sorrow for his friend who had fallen victim to it.

"Word is it was Trey's people," Burt continued. "You know Trey's in a wheel chair and can't walk now."

Sam had an answer to his concerns of the Trey Brownlee incident and was afraid this very thing would happen. He knew he could not express his true concerns to Jose about the issue as he could be very bullheaded at times. Now Trey had his revenge, but at what cost to him personally?

***

Jose's uncle had been the financial back for many of the projects he shared with Sam in his business endeavors. With Jose down and his uncle gone, Sam was unsuited financially to shelter the load of a DJ group and a strip club. Jose always had a steady flow of major cash to cover the expenses of the business when times were hard. Sam had to make the determination of cutting his losses and realigning his business prospects with something practical that could sustain his own livelihood. He knew he would definitely need to spend more time away now and was worried how it would affect his relationship with his wife. Now that he could not sustain her contempt with money, he wondered what more he could do.

Sam decided he would sell off all the assets he shared with Jose and take the proceeds to start a business he could successfully operate in a solo capacity. He initially felt hesitant in starting a strip club because it sucked money from the community with working fathers giving money away that could be put to more useful means and mothers paying club owners to walk around naked in their establishment. Morally was it the right thing to do? No. However, at the time Jose was fronting everything. The startup money for the business and all expenses associated to guarantee success were facilitated by him. It was a no-brainer for someone that was poor with scarce few avenues for advancement in this society. Sam was a friend of a big money boss and in his role all he had to do was support that clout.

Sam wondered if Trey had beef with him, considering he and Jose were best buddies since childhood. Trey himself had known them since he was younger also, but he had never been friendly with the pair. Trey would have to be vigilant and on his guard now. It was very unpredictable when it came to street justice and he could not afford to get caught up in a predicament.

***

Jose's crew and other business associates raged an all-out street fight against Trey's crew. Daily shootings occurred in various pockets of the city ending in deaths and maiming. The Centac 26 taskforce was formulated to combat the raise in violence during the increased spike in crime among the neighborhoods. Trey had simply gone underground as he could not take active participation in the violence due to his new found disability. But like every so called kingpin he called the shots from the rear.

Centac was everywhere locking up smugglers, users, gangbangers, prostitutes and bystanders.

A Korean investment group bought out the club and continued to run it as a nude cabaret in the community. The Koreans had an affiliation with the Miami Dade Chamber of Commerce and they were privy to many secret business deals throughout the city. Their investment group sent perspective employees, mostly family members, to work in their newly acquired organizations in America. In many of the black neighborhoods the money spent by its residents were pocketed by Korean businesses creating a symbiotic relationship.

Sam took the money from the deal and invested it in real estate; property was purchased along the Biscayne Boulevard, an area containing old seedy motels and retirement spots in Miami Beach. He had always heard that investing one's money in a house or some type of real estate venture would yield long term financial returns.

Being linked to Jose soon caught up with Sam though; he was arrested by Centac 26 with the use of the newly enacted RICO act. He was threatened with a 12-year bid for conspiracy in a criminal enterprise although he was never directly active in Jose's affairs. Jose was sentenced to over a decade of federal time.

***

Chapter 7: The Hustle

The killings related to the Trey Brownlee incident got the attention of local and national law enforcement. The city was awash with investigators from whatever alphabet group you could name. FBI, DEA, FDLE so on and so forth. Sam was in custody under the FDLE jurisdiction of Florida. He was heavily questioned by investigators looking to get a tip on Jose's operations. In a small elevator-sized office room investigators questioned Sam on Jose's operation hierarchy and layout.

"Who was Jose's contact?" said the first investigator.

There was a small table in the corner of the room in front of Sam's chair. The investigator pulled the wooden chair from the front end of the table and placed it in front of Sam. He sat face-to-face and Sam thought for sure the guy had smoked a zillion packs of menthol lights, had a tuna salad and drank gallons of coffee before the interview.

"Listen, I know nothing of Jose's business," Sam said sternly.

The room was padded with soft pads used by movers on elevator walls when moving heavy furniture in the downtown office buildings. There were no windows, but Sam knew others were observing due to the lone video camera high in the corner of the room. Sam had watched many episodes of the television show "Bad Boys" and could guess at the many tactics used by the investigators. The investigator wheezed as he tried intensifying his line of questioning; he was a portly sized man with apparent bad health.

"I am here of my own accord and my only knowledge of Jose's dealings was through our club business," Sam stated.

Another investigator entered the room as Sam finished his statement.

"Ease up on the guy, officer," said the second investigator.

Here it goes, the good cop, bad cop scenario, Sam thought to himself. He was waiting, betting himself that they were going to spring that overplayed technique. The second investigator entered and stood near the door as it shut behind him.

"Sam, we want to play it straight with you," he said.

"Give us what we want and we can cut a deal," he said.

"I didn't do nothing and I don't know nothing," said Sam adamantly.

The second investigator gave a kinda' snort and placed his hands on his waist like an old football coach dissatisfied with a call by a referee during game time.

"Cut him loose, Slick, it's been six hours. He ain't giving us nothing," he said to the seated investigator.

They both left the room and Sam could hear muttered curse words as they let the door slam behind them on their way out. Sam sat straight up in his chair and folded his arms patiently waiting to be released from the confines of the tiny room. He had not eaten and wondered about his wife, Vivian. Did she get a call? He decided against calling her because he knew he was not involved in Jose's criminal dealings. He sighed under his breath and waited for the cops to come back to the room to release him.

As he sat in the interview room he pondered on what he was going to do about the situation and how he would move on with his life after this incident. He was sure that he

117

had no interest in getting involved with Jose's business proposals moving forward. He was positive that he didn't want to fall back on working night and day in fast food. He realized the only thing he had going for himself was music. He would have to make a way with what he was good at and in what he was naturally inclined to excel. He was of the resolve that music would have to lay the path of his life's purpose.

***

Sam was happy to be out of the clutches of the cops and thought of the fate of Jose and his team of associates. He had known Jose from a young kid and realized that life had been hard for him on the streets. Jose had looked out for Sam when he had money and Sam respected that about him. True friends remain true despite money, women or other worldly things that could spark envy among men.

Sam walked briskly along the street from the police station precinct of downtown Miami. Dusk was beginning to fall over the city and he wanted to get home before it was dark. As he walked along the sidewalk, occasionally he would pick up a stone and skip it across the roadway. He had gone from riding in new top-of-the-line foreign automobiles to walking. The streets were deserted with the exception of a few cats scrounging around in garbage cans. This area of the city contained a lot of blighted areas and burned out buildings from the Miami riot fires of years past. It often took time for civil service workers, such as fire fighters to respond to resident area incidents.

As Sam walked home, he recalled the riots when the city was set ablaze by angry black men and women for the killing of a local insurance salesman. Police chased a black insurance salesman on a motorcycle and shot him misidentifying him for a common thug. The man was well respected in the neighborhood and the area erupted with a week-long riot. Businesses were burned, public buildings damaged and a few people were killed in the ruckus. It took days before the fires were doused and before control was regained by city officials.

The street lights were beginning to come on as Sam noticed the familiarity of his neighborhood. He wondered if his wife had started dinner because he was famished from his little adventure. He wondered if she had gotten word of the bust; he was in no mood to entertain questions. Vivian could be a real detective herself when it comes to finding out information on a matter about which she's passionate.

***

Sam found his food warm under a pot lid on the stove. The house was quiet, but he could hear the low murmur of the T.V. in the bedroom. She must be nodding in bed he thought to himself as he lifted a few bites of food from the plate to his mouth. He had forgotten about food as his hunger had taken a back seat to his vivid thoughts during his walk. He was unsure about his future now that Jose was out of the picture and he knew he had to rebound quickly from the situation he was facing. He had kept the DJ equipment stored away and since Jose would be busy with his legal problems the equipment would be his responsibility.

Sam decided to setup the equipment in a spare room of his home that was not being used and would convert it to a lightweight recording room. He would use the room as a studio for people interested in making songs.

It would be tough getting DJ gigs he thought to himself because he really didn't have a crew like Jose that could move the equipment. The money was good, but without Jose he knew he would have to pay anyone that he recruited for the job.

Many DJ groups in Miami were branching off into the hip hop music industry and Sam would follow the trend. It was very popular for the drug hustlers to funnel their profits into equipment, rap crews and talent shows. Their names would become big among neighborhood youths and garner street credibility. Fast cars, women and money were the things that made an average street peddler popular. Sam saw a void in regards to youth

desires in relation to their future and many

saw rap as a viable avenue. Sam decided if he

could build an operable crew he could

capitalize on the rap music thing.

***

Chapter 8: Baby Steps

Sam kept the DJ equipment in storage at his house and began remodeling a room to begin assembling a studio. He continued to Disc Jockey birthday parties for kids and family members before actively recruiting people to help him in his business. This was one thing that was his and he was confident at his ability to DJ. He had studied many of the successful people in his society and they were all good at what they do. In whatever endeavor they pursued, they were the best and Sam felt this way about his skills. While being a DJ was not a white collar job of privilege, it put money in his pocket.

"I hope you don't think that you're going to be playing that loud music in this house," said Vivian with an inquisitive expression on her face. She considered her home that of a family atmosphere and had no interest in having it converted to a night club environment. The life in music consists of late nights, binge drinking and other excesses.

"Babe, don't worry," said Sam. "I got this; it's only for temporary storage now." He knew that eventually the equipment would need to be moved. He would keep it here as long as possible until something developed where he could make a move. Sam sat at his desk in the corner of his apartment and contemplated his business strategy for bringing in business.

"Why don't you get Heavy Face to help you get parties," remarked Vivian. "He knows everyone in the neighborhood." Vivian was good for sparking ideas thought Sam to himself. He had always made it not known to her how valuable she was to him at times. One word or thought can sometimes lead to the development of major things. The journey of a thousand miles begins with one step he said to himself.

"Heavy Face is a social guy. I'm the business mind in this deal," said Sam sternly eyeing his wife as she walked through the room sparsely sweeping the floor. In moving his equipment, he had dropped threading and dirt over the entire floor. He was very meticulous about the cleanliness of his surroundings and appreciated her picking up after him.

"However, Heavy is my homie and he is going to help run the show," said Sam as he rose and walked from the room. He wanted to focus his thoughts and Vivian was starting to be a nag. She sometimes just didn't know when to stop he said with a chuckle to himself. Sam would use some of the money he saved from the club business and funnel it into building his music empire. Jose would be locked up for a few years and Sam knew that he couldn't count on his support financially.

***

"Yo, bring that fucking hose over here man," said Heavy Face. "You stupid or something?" Heavy Face stood in the center of a parking lot barking orders at a young skinny Haitian kid. The kid was new to the city and Heavy had just hired him on with his mobile car washing business. Many immigrants often come into Miami with no papers and they look for jobs that will pay under the table. The parking lot was in a shopping plaza not too far from the NFL football stadium. Young guys were pulling in with new Mercedes and Jaguars. They were obviously the rookie players who still try to come through the hood upon signing the big contracts.

Heavy Face ran with some goons that robbed drug dealers back in the day and he made his money. He stashed some dollars away and when that venture folded, he started his own mobile car wash business. Most guys in the city have a fallback business to survive the rough times. Because many guys get felonies from selling drugs, they must work under-the-table jobs. Having a lawn service, car wash, T-shirt shop or CD/DVD sales business are the usual choices.

"Yo Heavy, I heard your man got major time," said this guy with braided corn rows in his hair. He sat in a nearby plastic white chair. Heavy walked towards the guy while rolling a long water hose over his shoulder like a cowboy lasso.

"Who?" replied Heavy with an inquisitive look on his face. Sweat poured down his forehead from the work. He was still irritated from fussing with the Haitian kid and it showed in the expression on his face.

"Your man Jose who ran with that Sam cat in the city," the guy with the corn rows replied. He rocked back on the chair as he spoke. He wore a blue Dickies boy shorts set with blue converse and swatted himself from time-to-time with a light blue colored wash rag.

"Yeah," replied Heavy. "That's fucked up how he went out. You gotta look out for self, my man, in the game it's a solo venture,"

he said. "What the next man eats can't make

you shit and vice versa," said Heavy with a

faraway gaze in his eyes.

The guy sat nodding his head in the

affirmative as if he was in church. In black

southern churches the congregation gives

affirmations to the preacher when he hits on

certain important key points and this was one

of those cases.

"Looks like Sam will have to take over

operations," said the corn-rowed gentlemen.

"Naw," responded Heavy quickly. "He

ain't that type of cat. He was largely shielded

from that life by Jose," he said. "He ain't built

for it, but don't get me wrong he's 'bout his money," said Heavy with a grin.

"You think he kept it real and didn't snitch?" inquired the corn-rowed guy. "He was taken down with Jose, but he out now," he said. "I mean if that was his man and all, he should be riding with him," he said as he adjusted himself in the chair for a reply from Heavy Face.

"Man look-a-here," said Heavy with his hand extended out like a knife about to cut a cake suspended in mid air in front of him. "What does it matter, like I said before this is a dolo game. You gotta go for self," he reiterated.

"Yeah, all the major players are getting put in a pine box or on lock down," said the guy with the corn rows. "The game is changing man," he said.

"You right," replied Heavy. "That's why you have to have a backup plan." He removed the wrapped hose from around his shoulder and tossed it to the side. As a car pulled up to be serviced, he motioned for the driver to pull it into a nearby empty stall.

Heavy approached the car. "What you need, we got full service," he said. The windows of the red BMW were jet black. Heavy could not see thru them, so he had to wait for the person to lower them or exit the vehicle.

"What's up, Heavy Face," said the car occupant. It was Sam, "Give me the full job big player," he said closing the car door behind him. He gave Heavy Face a pound and the two exchanged greetings as onlookers watched.

"I got you my man," said Heavy. "You're in good hands at this car wash," he said.

Sam pulled Heavy aside and said, "Let me holler at you about some business for a minute." The two walked over the lot a bit and Sam placed his hand on Heavy's shoulder. He leaned in and in a hushed tone began speaking.

"Look, I got an idea for making some money in the music game and the plan is to do street DJ gigs. This will make the money to get a rap music label going and capitalize in Miami with this New York rap phenomena. It's just like selling dope, but instead it's music," said Sam. Sam paused to see what reaction Heavy had to what he heard. The car wash continued to buzz with people milling around waiting for their vehicles. The Haitian kid began vacuuming Sam's ride being careful not to call attention to him which could enrage Heavy.

"You think you can make some real money like in the dope game?" asked Heavy. Sam could see that Heavy was playing with the idea, but he needed more assurance.

"We did the DJ thing before and you know Jose made some nice loot with that," said Sam. "This rap music label will more than triple that and I think this thing will blow up in Miami." Heavy looked to the ground and rubbed his chin. His business did ok, it got him by, but he wanted big money like he once had back in the day. He knew that Sam was sincere in making big money and he did well when he ran with Jose.

"I'm in man, sign me up!" said Heavy.

Sam was delighted to hear Heavy was on board for the venture. He knew Heavy was a soldier and would do what it took to get things done. Sam was aware of the street code and this code often times was a selfish one.

The culture cultivated the idea that the strong were kings of the jungle and the weak were prey. Any sign of weakness called for exploitation by those in power positions or by perceived bosses. Those that had a common cause and interest ran in packs like beasts of the wild and attacked in the same manner as well.

Sam reminisced on the story of the scorpion and the frog. The scorpion pleaded with a frog to carry him across a communal pond and the frog refused on fear that the scorpion may poison him. After the scorpion assured the frog that he wouldn't, the amphibian agreed. As the frog carried the insect on his back and approached the center of the pond he felt a burning sensation. The frog turned and asked the scorpion, "Why did you sting me when you said you wouldn't?"

The scorpion replied, "That's what I do. I'm a scorpion."

Human nature is the key to understanding and Sam knew Heavy had a heart.

***

Chapter 9: The Dream

Sam desired more than just making money and being rich, he wanted to build something meaningful. He mostly wanted to build an organization and that would mean a lot of steady hard work. He knew that he would have to develop a team and a plan to pursue this dream of his. He was done with the street hustle and also the strip club business. Strip clubs for owners are marvelous and they make tons of money. Hard working black men and ballers go there to live out unfulfilled dreams by throwing money at young women. Such money could be used to do much more in neighborhood communities, but instead is wasted in 'make it rain' contests for establishing reputations.

Sam had performed extensive research and noted trends within the city among the youth. He discovered that music, rumors, fashion, food and religion were all a major part of the Black culture. His angle would be music and from that he would branch out into all other ventures. He knew if he could craft a good business plan, he could grasp his dreams by the horns.

"You're always dreaming and planning," said Vivian.

She had grown accustomed to seeing Sam mull over situations and problems while sipping cognac. She noticed he especially enjoyed the Hennessy brand.

"You would be much happier if you lived in the present," she said. "Without the present there can be no future."

Sam lounged in his arm chair with his drink in hand and jingled the glass making the ice clink against the sides of the goblet. He liked Vivian's attempt at challenging his intellect, she could be deep sometimes he thought to himself. Her words rang in his mind like a bell and he explored the meaning of its intent. It could be possible that she was seeking attention and seeing how she could get some sort of a rouse.

Vivian continued to busily clean while Sam was seated; he placed his drink on a nearby stand and pulled her down to him. She sat in his lap and squirmed a bit. He whispered in her ear and she stopped squirming. He kissed her on the cheek and nestled his head against her warm body. This is worth working for he said to himself.

***

Sam organized his Dj business with a top-down management style. He structured his company similarly to how many of the twentieth century big businesses had operated. He was the CEO and the founder along with Heavy Face who would be the VP of operations and management. Heavy led recruitment and had guys from the neighborhood on staff for day-to-day operations.

Heavy continued to run his own mobile car wash, but instead of being there daily he hired someone to manage his business. Sam coordinated calendar dates and met with individuals interested in scheduling party times. Heavy managed maintenance and setup of DJ equipment and the logistics for getting to locations. The business was sound, organized and professional. All members had business cards, T-shirts and Polo shirts that promoted the business.

With the business making good profits, Sam and Heavy successfully set up a one stop shop for music in a local flea market. The business expanded to selling mix tapes as well as doing parties for the local neighborhood residents. Sam successfully made essential contacts in the music industry by partnering with local radio personalities at community festivals. Heavy was more of a hands-on street hustler and he ran all personnel matters.

While doing a party in the neighborhood, Sam was introduced to a host of amateur rappers who were very young in age. Sam made note of a couple of the youngsters and told them of his plan to get in the rap business. They seemed interested in Sam's plan and he made a conscientious effort to let them rap on the microphone whenever he did community parties.

"Yo Heavy, I'm short a hundred dollars on my pay this week," said one of the DJ's.

He was known as Smurf among his friends due to his dark complexion. He was often teased because people said he looked blue black when the sunlight hit him the right way. He had entered the one stop shop at the flea market early that day and waited an hour until Heavy opened up for business.

"Smurf, you know you were late twice last week," Heavy replied.

A Black and Mild cigar dangled from his lips as he spoke with irritation in his voice. He had always had trouble with Smurf for minor infractions and conduct while on the job. He could see Smurf was a problem and he was unsure how to handle the guy.

"Yeah, but that's too much money to take from somebody for being late," said Smurf in anger.

"That's the policy," said Heavy in a curt manner.

He continued opening the shop with his back turned to Smurf. Smurf stood silent and watched Heavy prepare the shop for the day's business activities. He was breathing hard and Heavy was ready for whatever the situation called for as he remained aware of Smurf's presence.

Smurf turned and walked away.

"It's like that Heavy?" he commented.

"Yes Sir," said Heavy as he continued working in the shop.

Sam telephoned the shop as he did daily to discuss business with Heavy and was surprised to hear what happened with Smurf. Sam knew Smurf from the neighborhood and although he ran with some goons he was a good hustler. Hindsight told Sam he should have gone to the shop, but he had a couple of appointments that he needed to solidify for business.

"You need me to come in today?" he said to Heavy.

"I got this," said Heavy ending the call abruptly.

As Heavy continued with his daily routine two men entered the shop. They browsed the music catalogue and asked for DJ rates. Heavy was well known in the community and knew many individuals. He was unfamiliar with the gentlemen and felt caution. There was a nearby iron on the shop shelves and Heavy eyed it for a moment. In that split moment one guy pulled a gun and Heavy grabbed the iron throwing it. The guy with the gun pulled the trigger shooting Heavy in the chest, Heavy fell back from the blast of the shot hitting the back wall. The iron successfully struck the man that wasn't armed leaving a gash in his head as he stumbled, reeling at the sight of his own blood gushing.

People in the flea market began yelling and running for the exit. The shooter took off leaving his partner on the floor bleeding from his injury.

"Somebody get help!" yelled a burly bald headed guy with gold teeth in his mouth.

The scene was chaotic and in the ruckus the wounded attacker had gotten to his feet and wandered away from the ghastly scene. The blood covered the floor like bright red carpet and people jumped the pools of fluid as they stampeded. The security guard finally appeared on the scene out of breath with his gun still holstered.

"What happened? Which way they went?" he inquired.

His questions were drowned out by the sounds of people talking loudly, shouting and bustling about the floor of the market. Other vendors began closing their shops hoping to dash out before the police could arrive to begin lengthy questioning of the events. In all the frenzied activity no one thought to check on Heavy's vitals. His body came to life on the floor jerking as he violently coughed up syrupy pools of blood. As the outdoors of the flea market opened with people exiting, the sirens of the emergency response professionals could be heard.

***

Sam entered the hospital and could see the lobby crowded with the neighborhood street regulars and Heavy Face's family members. Paramedics were wheeling Heavy in on a gurney and they swiped right past Sam. As the gurney passed, Heavy grabbed Sam and slipped him a key.

"Black Caddy," said Heavy as he collapsed onto the padded cot.

He was wheeled in to the emergency room among wales of agonizing cries and yells of loved ones milling around the hospital lobby.

Sam stood in the lobby of the hospital still holding the blood stained keys he had gotten from Heavy. He was unsure what the whole exchange meant. Why would Heavy be concerned about a set of keys after being shot and almost dying? He walked out the lobby and people continued to arrive asking questions and speculating on how the event occurred. The commotion seemed to fade from Sam's mind as he walked. It seemed as if everything was now moving in slow motion and the sound of the atmosphere muted with only his thoughts being heard. He walked and soon found his legs running carrying him away from the hectic scene.

***

Sam found himself back at the flea market and he held the blood stained keys in his hands uncertain of what action to take. In the back alley of the shop The Cadillac driven by Heavy was parked. It was an older model car with vogue tires and a glistening new black gloss paint job; the car was in great condition.

Sam opened the car and looked over the black leather interior. He ran his hand over the seats and over the floorboards. He popped the trunk and walked around to the back of the car to take a look inside. He could not believe what he was looking at and quickly looked around to see if anyone saw him. The trunk had a huge clear zip locked brick of money in it and Sam could view only big bills that looked new.

Sam got a call while at the shop and the news was that Heavy had died due to a massive amount of blood loss. He was alone and not sure what to do with the business.

How could he move on without Heavy and what would he do with the money in Heavy's car? He didn't think Heavy was in the drug game.

He rationed that many guys with felony charges were suspicious about banks and kept their money in hiding places. He thought this could be the case with Heavy and he reasoned he wanted the money to go to good use. Sam decided he would realize the dream he shared with Heavy and make his death have a meaning. He would dedicate the money to building an organization in the memory and dream of Heavy Face.

Heavy had grown up in a rough area of Miami and his will to grind for money had made him successful in his own right. He also had affiliations with gang, drug and criminal members which often were a detriment. When growing up in the hood, you go to school and church with the people that grow into these figures. It's sometimes hard to disassociate with them when they have known you all their lives. This was Heavy's circumstance thought Sam in his analysis of the situation.

Heavy caught a felony charge being in the wrong place at the wrong time and with the wrong group of people. He learned then that associations can determine the trajectory of your life. He had left those associations and started his own entrepreneurial endeavors which sustained him in life. Sam associated with Heavy because he had proven himself as an able entrepreneur and his connections in the neighborhood were invaluable.

Sam's heart was heavy from the loss, but he would make good with the last wishes of Heavy. The people that murdered him only made a martyr which would inspire the youth.

***

Chapter 10: Jail House Rap

Sam set out to talent scout using the money he got from Heavy. He would find a young artist and work with them to reach his goal of establishing a successful business. Chain Link Records would be the name Sam would use for his record company business. Sam recruited two groups from the neighborhood that he was familiar with while doing DJ gigs for parties. The money found in the trunk of the car amounted to ten thousand dollars and Sam sunk it all into the business.

Sam set out to assemble a studio in the rear of the DJ one stop shop located in the flea market. He knew he needed a good quality condenser microphone and preamplifier combo. He decided to get one from Dan's Music Shop. Dan's was a well known shop in North Miami that catered to music entrepreneurs in the hood.

"What's up, Dan?" said Sam as he entered the music store.

Dan was a Jamerican and his family was from the island of Jamaica. He was born and raised in Miami and his parents were immigrants from Kingston. He sat on a stool behind a long glass counter with long dreadlocks coiled down his back. Dan made huge profits making sales on high-end speakers and top grade amplifiers.

"I need a good mic and preamp combo for eight hundred dollars, preferably AKG brand," stated Sam.

He knew that AKG made good quality inexpensive products and he wanted to get the best buy on a shoe string budget. The long glass counter was filled with expensive microphone set ups and the price tags were out of Sam's desired range. In the music equipment world, the quality of sound is directly related to the quality of the equipment chosen to do the work.

"I got just what you need," Dan replied. "Give me a minute," he said before shuffling off into the back of the store.

The store was sparsely decorated with professional grade music equipment under show cases and bass bin speaker setups aligned the walls. Not many customers were in the store, but Sam knew the store's clientele spent thousands of dollars in one purchase. Dan appeared again carrying a see-through case with the mic combo. Its chrome parts sparkled as the lights inside the store shined down on it and Sam instantly knew he wanted it.

"Gimmie' a grand and it's yours," he said as he placed it on the glass top counter.

"I'll tell you what," said Sam with a slight hesitation. "Throw in a compressor and EQ for twelve hundred," countered Sam.

It's a deal," replied Dan eagerly shaking Sam's already extended hand.

***

Sam got his first string rap crew to help him assemble the studio back at the shop. He had gotten a few foam panels to align the walls to proof against the boxy sounds that often seep into a track when doing recordings. Sam was careful not to go overboard with the foam because he knew it could lead to dullness in the sound's quality.

"Yo Sam, where should we set this up at?" said one of the youth of the first string rap crew.

Sam realized that the correct placement of the foam was essential in providing

professional sound quality in the dampening
of sound. He took the foam out of the young
man's hand and centered it on the wall. Same
wanted it in the correct spot so as to soak up
most of the sound generated from studio
sessions. He also wanted the studio to have a
professional appearance; such would give the
impression that this was a serious venture.

"See what I've done," he remarked.
"Make all the placement of foam like I've just
done on this wall."

The group worked feverishly to get the
components of the studio in place. They
wanted to get to work making songs as soon as
possible. They didn't know that Sam had a
pre-planned lecture already prepared to cover

the organization's goals and each of their individual contributions towards making a successful group debut on the record label.

"Ok guys, I know you've been busting you humps to get this thing done," said Sam. "First thing is that we want crisp clear vocals, so we stand 10 to 14 inches away from the mic when we record."

Sam wanted to establish this trademark sound for the Chain Link brand. He hoped that anything produced by his business be recognized by that style. Sam determined that because of his experience in the streets of Miami with his partner Jose, Gangsta Rap was the most appropriate. He would relay the stories in rhyme vicariously through Jose. He decided to write the songs and have his signed artist recite the raps.

"Let's talk contracts," said Sam as he clapped his hands together and began rubbing them.

The lead member of the First String Rap Crew did most of the negotiations for the group and had known Sam from the neighborhood for years. Sam desired to be an astute business man and he wanted to be seen as a fair person that wished to empower his folks. He wanted to succeed and prosper by helping others do the same.

"Listen, you can keep your masters and we split everything 50/50," he said. "You can keep your publishing and all that will be included in the contracts in print. The only thing I want you to do is make bomb-ass music," said Sam.

The guys were astounded at the deal Sam offered and quickly gave a verbal agreement to the proposal set before them. It was rare that a music label would grant ownership to publishing and masters' rights. The group could use this opportunity to establish a real business legacy for themselves and future descendants. Sam was a real nigga' and that's how he would project the image of the company among his competitors in the business.

Sam had been secretly meeting with a distribution company trying to ink a deal and he wanted to have contracts established to solidify the venture. The guys had no problem with signing the contracts and Sam was ready to launch his business. The deal would give the company nationwide access to a market that could generate millions for the business.

***

Sam sat in an engineering studio in Atlanta and had brought in a set of tracks for songs that would be mixed for pressing. He never truly understood this part of the business and thought he would sit in on the session. The studio was immaculately decked with Shape Audio speakers in each corner of the room. The lights on the digital recording boards danced as if to their own beat and low oxygen cables ran along the side corners of the equipment panels. Sam sat behind one of the giant SSL 4000 boards with the Engineer and watched him work the levers.

"Do you work often with Pro Tools?" Sam asked.

"On certain tracks I do," replied the engineer.

Sam was fond of the sound quality of the 808 beat making processes and would seek to have it incorporated in his projects. Miami music was home of the bass and southern rappers often incorporated the effects into their genre of music. The engineer began pitching the EQ as he added drums and smoothed out the baseline on one particular track of Sam's.

Sam's eyes darted over the controls recording the movements of the man.

"What's the real purpose of hiring an engineer?" asked Sam in an inquisitive manner.

"For one, with one main engineer it cuts down on your music being bootlegged. Secondly, for a professional industry standard sound, hiring an engineer is essential," he replied. "It all depends on what sound you're looking for," he added.

As they sat in the studio mixing down the tracks, Sam had the engineer bounce a few of the tracks to stereo and then loaded in Pro Tools. The song synced inline and had a professional sound equipped with a ferocious base line. Sam bobbed his head as his co-pilot let one of the tracks play out over the studio speakers. They continued to work for hours as vocals on the tracks were edited, compressed and layered for maximum sound effects.

Various rap artists and their entourages roamed the studio with women. Alcohol and weed flowed freely as groups prepared to lay tracks in the recording booths. Sam was accustomed to this type of environment. The studios in Miami sometimes played host to strippers in the late hours of a recording session. No matter where you go some things often times remain the same thought Sam to himself. He noticed many of the ATL artists wore the same kind of gold chain around their necks. Some record companies often establish a logo or symbol for their artists to rally around. Sam rationalized the act was a morale booster and a useful tool of control for some.

Sam was here on business and he decided he had plenty of opportunities for fun later. He would focus on learning all he could about the business of music. Many engineers clam up when asked questions about their work and this engineer was eager to expound upon the knowledge he possessed of the system. Sam sat childlike with his ears tuned and asked as many questions as he could think of about the process.

***

Chapter 11: Friends

Sam entered the lockup at Miami Dade Detention Center and felt a bit nervous upon walking into the building. He was directed to walk through the security scanner and it started to beep as he exited the other side. The policeman that worked the machine motioned Sam over and directed him to remove anything consisting of metal from his pockets. He was then directed to the visitor's room and escorted to a room filled with people who sat around square tables with stools on each side. The room felt cold and the walls were painted pasty white like a hospital room.

"Who are you here for, sir?" inquired a young woman passing out reading material.

"A childhood friend of mine," replied Sam courteously smiling at the woman.

The woman offered Sam a newspaper, but he declined it. He was more focused on his meeting with Jose. It had been almost sixteen months since he had been sentenced and Sam was unsure how Jose felt about being in prison. Did he blame me for not having his back? Sam often questioned himself. Maybe if I had participated in that lifestyle to the extent he did, I could have helped him avoid his fate Sam pondered.

"What's up, homeboy?"

Sam was still pondering his thoughts when he thought he heard someone speak to him. He was seated at one of the square tables in the back of the room on a stool. His head was bowed with his hands clasp on the top of the table and he looked up to see who was greeting him. It was Jose standing in front of him in street clothes.

"What up, man?" Sam replied.

The two men shook hands and gave each other half hugs before seating themselves on the stools by the square table. Jose seemed to be in good spirits and looked good considering he had been locked down for over a year. Many cats get depressed and stop eating thinking that their lives are over, but Jose seemed full of life.

"How you doing in here, man?" Sam asked.

The room was now filled with inmates talking with their guests and the atmosphere was busy with conversations. Prison officers walked the isles of the tables to ensure no contraband or other unsavory deed was occurring. The visitation seemed more relaxed than Sam had expected, but the probation officers made their presence known.

"It's better than I expected. We usually wear scrubs, but they let us wear our regular clothes for visitations or court appearances," said Jose. "They got me housed in F unit, any newbie that's in process goes there," he stated.

"How's your lifestyle here?" Sam asked.

"Well, when I first got here I was given two envelopes and paper to write letters and I was allowed to pick books and magazines to put in a cell. They tested me for HIV and any other disease before taking DNA samples." Jose said. "I was expecting it to be like prisons in the movies, but it's very different."

Sam could see that Jose had no problem adapting to his situation and wanted to get an insight on his feelings of what had occurred leading to his arrest.

"Man, I feel guilty; I was there with you with all the women and parties. Now I'm free, you're not," said Sam.

"Man, don't sweat that shit, we grown men," replied Jose a bit irritated. "If you gonna' do the crime, you best be ready to do the time," he said. "I'm a soldier and I take chances. You successfully appealed your conviction and beat it with the use of the best lawyers. I manned up to mines and that's it."

Sam respected Jose's words and knew that he meant what he said. Jose was not the kind of person that lied. He was also not a snitch and had no interest in the 5k1 or rule 35 plea. He had no reason for not being straight with a person and his character is of a good nature despite his current predicament. Jose was a true friend regardless of the difference in race, morality, economic status or any other demographic society places on individuals.

"I heard you started a record label," stated Jose.

Sam appeared surprised Jose knew about his activities. He didn't realize Jose continued to have outside knowledge of action in the neighborhood despite his incarceration. Was he still dabbling and who was the outside source? He thought to himself. He was unsure how Jose was receiving his updates and was quite sure he knew about what happened to Heavy Face.

"Yeah, I got some guys I'm working with," replied Sam. "We plan to do some songs on you and how you put work in for Dade County."

"Yeah," said Jose with a chuckle.

"You cool with that? I got you're commissary. I'm your boy." Sam stated.

"As long as you keep it real and true to life, it's no problem," replied Jose. "You know the story and we been friends for a long time. I respected our friendship and have not pressured you into anything you weren't comfortable with." Jose commented.

Jose's accent was thick, but it sometimes sounded funny when he tried to speak in slang using certain types of Miami street vernacular.

Sam noticed he looked out of place in the cold

drab settings of the white prison walls. He was

accustomed to viewing Jose in the light of

pizzazz, settings with a backdrop of flowing

wine, women and luxury cars. The saying

goes 'hard ballers fall hard' and Jose seemed

unfazed with his fall from grace. Sam could

see times were changing from the highlife he

experienced while running with Jose's crew.

With this new endeavor he hoped to document

those experiences for a new upcoming

generation of youth. Sadly to say, by the time

Jose would see the light of day it would be an

entirely new millennia.

"So, whenever you need a refresher on

stories, come see me," said Jose.

"That's all I need to hear, homeboy," stated Sam.

***

Chapter 12: The Fork in the Road

Sam was determined to be successful as a business entrepreneur and he negotiated a distribution deal for the albums his company produced. The distribution deal would allow the records to be manufactured and distributed in wholesale to any retailer. Sam sold the records for the wholesale price less the negotiated distribution fee that covered the distributor's overhead expense. The distribution fee was arranged from 18% to 25% and the balance of the payment went to the business. Cassette tapes were wholesaled at $5.00 with a 25% distribution fee which amounts to $3.75 per cassette. Sam calculated that if he sold 270,000 copies he could make

$1,012,500.00 in profits for the business.

The music industry recognition of

record sales is the standards of gold, platinum

and diamond. Gold is the sale of records that

amount to 500,000 units which is the least

amount of sales to be recognized as a success

in the industry. Platinum is one million in

sales of units distributed to industry

consumers. Diamond recognition is the sale of

10,000,000 copies to consumers and represents

domination of the market.

Sam put out the group's first album and

sold just over 300,000 copies. It was well

received by the music critics but fell short of a

gold certified record. He had used the money

that Heavy Face left him to get the company started. The money he made with the album's sales went to paying the artist and cover company expenses for producing the album. He had made a pretty good profit in solidifying the distribution deal with the company.

Sam was recognized in the industry as an independent record label. If he had signed the group to a major deal, there would be less money to go around. The more middle men involved in a project translates to more expenditure. However, with a major label, greater exposure is possible because of the expanded marketing budget. The access to a wider market of consumers can increase the notoriety of a music group. It must also be understood that notoriety doesn't always result in profit.

Sam utilized the profit from the album sales to invest into real estate and business ventures to increase his money for future endeavors. He planned to also begin work on a follow up album with the group and to work with the new artists he had in the pipe line for future album releases. Sam soon found himself living the life he dreamed with his improved living conditions the money brought to him.

"What happened last night? I thought we were going to dinner," said Vivian.

She stood over Sam's side of the bed looking impatient as she waited for his answer. Sam lay in bed with his clothes on from the night before. He could feel his head throbbing from a massive headache and his stomach felt a bit queasy. He had partied all night and had not realized he was due to take Vivian out for dinner.

"What?" he grumbled trying to think of an adequate lie to fend her off.

"I waited up expecting a call or something from you," she said.

Sam could hear the clock on his night stand ticking as he lay on the bed trying to remember last night. It seemed things were one big whirlwind since putting out the record and getting his business going. His schedule was instantly filled with invites to parties, video shoots, golfing tournaments and birthday parties. Sam felt that networking would certainly be good for growing his business and learning the intricate details of the music business landscape. He was certain he did not want to grow the business too large too quickly because he didn't want to lose control.

"Forget it!" exclaimed Vivian as she stormed out the bedroom.

Sam could hear her stomp down the hallway and he cringed as his head rung from the violent vibrations of the interaction. Her hostile energy had quickened the flow of blood within him and it shot straight to his head making his headache worse. He groaned drifting off to sleep again and the clock on the nearby night stand continued to tick and tock, tick and tock.

***

Sam could feel change coming into his life and he was unsure of how to deal with it. His environment was changing and this was demanding he change in order to conform to its parameters. Who could he confide in to deal with the anxiety he felt? Vivian was not speaking to him and he was not one to open up easily to those around him. He had set out to build and establish a legacy and now that he was beginning to realize that dream he felt apprehension.

Sam entered the one stop shop at the flea market and he proceeded to the office to field phone calls to start his business day. He had the group on a promotional tour to push record sales and was the only one in the office. The flea market was busy that afternoon and was a bit noisy with people bustling around. Sam pondered a while wondering if he should relocate into a more exclusive area for the home location of the organization.

Sam heard the front door of the shop open as the customer bell chimed alerting him of a visitor. He entered the lobby to find a tall blond with well-rounded curves wearing a form fitting red dress. She held a Valor purse on one arm and a notepad under the other.

Outside of local artists, delivery people and individuals looking for the Haitian restaurant next door the shop got few visitors.

"Hi, I'm Charlotte Finely from Bandstand Magazine," she said.

Sam noticed the woman wore a business suit and was very professional in her mannerisms. He was always attracted to women of that nature, but they seemed to always have a fleeting interest in him. Her blond hair flowed down to her shoulders and her heels made her seem taller than what she actually was.

"What can I help you with, Ms. Finely?" replied Sam.

"Please, call me Charlotte," she said. "I'm looking to talk with P-Man Sam about his recent distribution deal and upcoming album."

"Well, you got me," said Sam. "I'm always free for an interview with the media," he replied.

***

Just as the money and the recognition of the business were reaching its peak Sam could sense that something was due to go awry. He had an eerie feeling before leaving his home after breakfast and he had the same feeling on his drive to a couple of preset meetings on South Beach to discuss additional

191

marketing plans for the ongoing group tour.

He entered the lobby of the marketing firm and

bumped into one of the members of First String

rap group.

"What's happening, Boss?" said the

young rapper.

"What you doing here?" asked Sam.

"I wanted to catch you and give you a

heads up," said the young rapper looking

around. "The crew has decided to hire a

lawyer and they want a thorough review of the

contract before signing on to do the second

album." He stated.

This puzzled Sam because he took these

guys from nothing and established something

of them. It seemed a slap in the face to him, to

bring in an outsider, to evaluate a business deal from which they both prospered. Sam returned home and sat at his work desk contemplating on the news that the group took on an attorney. He soon received a call from the attorney on the terms of the second album contract. Sam made it clear to the attorney that if they didn't sign then fuck them. However, he made the comment out of anguish and little did he know the lawyer had the group on speaker phone. They heard the entire tirade.

In the months to come the group seldom participated in marketing activities for the current album and all talk on a second album was nonexistent. Sam rarely spoke with the crew and promotion activities came to a halt.

It seemed the sails of Sam's record company had lost all air and things were adrift.

In the meantime, he had established a good relationship with Charlotte Finely during the interview session about the album. She had founded the Bandstand Magazine and made it known she was looking for a business partner as the magazine needed a new direction. He knew little about journalism, but contemplated the idea. He knew a lot about the Black culture of Hip Hop and was well connected in his community. Sam felt he could bring a new perspective to the plight of young Blacks in his community.

***

Chapter 13: A New Start

The group members of First String were not happy with Sam and they let it be known by missing recording sessions. Sam didn't give into any concessions with the crew and continued to interact with them like business as usual. He was pissed that they now acted as if they ran the show and called the shots for the company. Sam decided to meet with the attorney of the group to get more of an insight into what was going on with them.

The attorney's office was located in a posh building on the corner of Brickell Avenue downtown Miami. It was a high rise skyscraper with a parking deck and guards that coordinated parking outside the lower level of the building. Sam parked his ride and proceeded to enter the building to meet with the attorney. The interior of the building was immaculately designed with art deco decorum and the lobby floor consisted of marble. Sam took the elevator up to the top floor and stepped into the office corridor. He was immediately acknowledged by an assistant who ushered him into the meeting with the waiting attorney.

"Glad for you to have joined us, Mr. Silvasteen," said the lawyer.

"Sure thing," replied Sam. He wanted to get this affair over as soon as possible.

They sat around an oak table with a pitcher of water and a couple of glasses centered in its middle. A secretary and two other attorneys were present. The room was a spacious high ceiled area with pictures of the building's architecture strong along the walls.

"Contracts are in place for the second album and the group has an additional stipulation for larger advances," said the attorney that greeted Sam as he entered.

"Advances were agreed upon before the group started doing business with the company and besides they're nonnegotiable," he replied as he sat in the oak stained chair across from his hosts.

The details of the contract were explained in detail and Sam had decided early on that he would not sign it. As he sat in the room listening to the rambling of the attorneys he thought of Charlotte and lamented of being in the predicament he was with the group.

***

Sam proceeded to Bandstand Magazine after his appointment with the attorney and now sat at the desk of Charlotte Finley. Her office, located in a shopping plaza not far from Interstate I95, was tiny and unassuming. It was mostly a two-person operation as she was just starting off as a business entity, but she had a year of experience in journalism.

"If you come aboard, we'll be partners 50/50," explained Charlotte.

"Great, with my business ideas and your journalistic background we could be a formidable force in this industry," said Sam.

The business was fairly new and she worked with an assistant in conducting the day-to-day activities of the organization. Sam decided to use his connections in the music business to allow Charlotte access in interviewing top- level management personnel. Sam's schedule was tight and his time was consumed with social networking events. His relationship with Vivian became extremely strained and his spare time went to socializing with Charlotte in building their media business.

"Are you going to the MTV awards show with me?" Charlotte inquired.

"I haven't decided yet," replied Sam.

He was torn between spending the evening at home or doing more networking at the show. He knew that his marriage was in trouble and he wanted to take steps to preserve it. MTV was a new video phenomenon and many celebrities were active in participating in its social ventures. It would be a good atmosphere in exposing the business profile.

"I'm looking to get a few excellent interviews for executive profile stories I'm running in the next print series of the magazine," said Charlotte.

She riffled through her rolodex as a copy of last month's print copy of the Bandstand Magazine lay upon her desk. She had made it a task to improve its reader content on every print run and believed that the MTV coverage could be a boost to sales. Sam resolved that he would not attend the event, but he would not tell Charlotte of his intentions. He didn't want to appear ambivalent about attending another networking function, so he would just lead her on until the last minute.

"I'm headed out, I'll give you a heads

up, if I go," said Sam as he dashed out the door.

Sam walked to his car in deep thought and upon his drive through the city decided to stop by the shop to work on some business before heading to the house. He felt alone in his business ventures and reminiscent on the days of his partnership with friends. Those were the good ole days he thought to himself. Now his friends were locked up or dead. He was lucky to have escaped such a fate and sometime took it for granted.

As he drove, he heard the tunes on the radio station Hot105 and the DJ was announcing the next radio spin being played. Sam turned the knob of the volume and First

String's new album single was played for the first time on that radio station. It felt good knowing that the work he put into the group was finally bearing fruit.

At the shop Sam checked the answering machine and sorted the mail. He contemplated on squashing the beef he had with the group, but wasn't going to make the first move. They owed him he felt. He was the one to risk his hard-earned money on their success. They should be grateful to him he reasoned. His thoughts were interrupted when he heard the pedestrian alert signal in the front office go off. Sam entered the front office and spied a gentleman in a dark suit and a derby hat.

"Can I help you?" Sam asked.

"Sam Silvasteen?" the man replied.

"Yeah," he replied.

"You've been served," the man said to Sam as he slapped the paper in Sam's hand and quickly exited the front entrance.

Sam stood in bewilderment for a couple of minutes before looking over the paperwork the man left in his hand. He was hopeful and wishing this wasn't what he thought it was. He had simply had enough at this point.

***

Sam sat parked in his car outside the magazine office located in one of the plazas of downtown Miami. In his lap, he held a pint of Hennessey cognac in a light colored paper bag he had gotten from a nearby package store. It was a rainy night and the streets were wet.

The black top of the parking lot gleamed in the

moonlight as the water ran across its surface.

Sam drank from the bottle he had in his lap

and watched the cars dart up and down the

street. He marveled at how the rain made the

atmosphere seem tropical. The skies were

clear and the warm weather was natural to the

climate during this time of year. The alcohol

burned the inside of Sam's throat as he gulped

it down straight with no chaser. He could feel

the effects of it as it warmed his belly. He was

getting blitzed now and his worries melted

away with each gulp. A white Jaguar pulled

up to the front of the office building and shut

off its headlights. Sam, temporarily blinded,

squinted his eyes from the bright light and then realized it was Charlotte.

"What you doing? What happened? You didn't call," she exclaimed.

She walked around to the passenger door and pulled the door open. She ducked into the car and slid into the passenger seat shutting the door. Sam could tell she had been drinking, he could smell the scent of merlot mixed with her perfume.

"Rough night, I couldn't bear the crow," said Sam.

"Want a swig," said Sam offering the bottle to her.

She took it, sipped and let out a gagging cough.

"I can't believe people like that stuff," she commented.

Sam chuckled. He wondered how it would be to mix business with pleasure; he turned his car engine on and pulled out of the parking lot.

***

Chapter 14: The Interview

Sam felt as if he was being squeezed out of the music business due to him being unable to sign his artists to do a second follow up album. However, a fortunate opportunity opened up for him as a journalist and business owner. Sometimes a selected path may lead a person down another road which may be what's divinely prophesied and Sam understood this as destiny. He decided to make the best of his opportunity and would exploit his departure with group members.

Sam made a phone call and contacted the group for a meeting in the neighborhood. He decided to interview them as a feature in the magazine in which he was now a journalist. He would set up in Carol City and explain how the group was formulated before making their music for production.

"I'm doing an interview with First String in the hood, want to come?" Sam asked.

"I think it's a guy thing, I am good," replied Charlotte with a chuckle.

"What, you scared to hang out in the black neighborhood," said Sam.

"Not at all, just not today for the interview," said Charlotte.

Sam wanted to expose Charlotte to the way rap artists thought about the industry and reveal their motivations for making music. He could sympathize with her not wanting to do the interview with him. She was still new to the gritty part of urban media and he would have to carry the line on developing that part of the business.

The interview was set up at an annual event called 'Jazz in the Garden' in Carol City. The group was due to open for a couple of other major groups and agreed to do the interviews backstage before going on to perform. Sam knew the group members intimately and believed he could get a breaking story that would increase readership for the organization. They felt comfortable with Sam because they knew him, but the issue about doing a second album was still a source for sore relations.

Sam departed the office and arrived on-site for the interview. He proceeded to the main stage careful to avoid the forming crowd for the event. He moved freely through security due to his media credentials. He liked having the access he was privy to due to his occupation as a reporter and found it made him feel a sense of power. This power was different from being a head executive with a rap label and was more professional to him for some unknown reason.

"What's up, Chief?" said one of the members of First String as Sam advanced to them through the throng of people.

The stage was filled with workers and industry people milling around before the performance start. All the members were present and they addressed Sam with respect. They had not spoken with him since the discussion concerning the album and were interested in what he had to say pertaining to the issue.

"Let's find a space to do the interview," Sam said to them.

"Let's go to the dressing room," said one of the members.

The dressing room was a makeshift closet of a structure that was put temporarily for the performers. It was sparsely decorated with a few chairs located in the center of the room. As the guys got settled Sam let them know off the bat how things were going to go between them.

"Look guys, we had an issue with doing a second album and I'm over that. I'm not one to hold artists hostage and in this business that's the way it goes. You're free to do what you want and I wish you success. As for now, this is an interview for a magazine feature which could be good exposure for you." Sam stated.

All the members respected what Sam had to say and were cool with proceeding with the interview. They spoke candidly about their motivations for becoming rap artists and the past history which dictated what they spoke about in their music. Sam recorded the interview on tape as well as took notations on what was being said. He wondered what he could use to break a major story concerning this interview as he questioned the crew.

Sam believed it was a conflict of interest to run the story as the crew had done recordings under his rap music label. He was unsure how to proceed with printing the interview in the upcoming addition of the magazine printing process, so he killed the story. He got word that the crew was not happy with his actions. They made derisive statements to associates in the music industry and to other reporters about him. Sam responded in kind and the rift between the two was exasperated by a war of words.

Sam sat at his desk in the shop and made a couple of business calls related to his music label business. He wanted to shut down business operations as smoothly as he had begun them and was ready to transition out of the game. He had made a pretty good profit and was looking at other business investments that could make him income. He was finishing up some paperwork before heading home when his phone rang.

"Collect call from Dade County Jail," said the operator. "Do you accept the charges?"

"Yes," replied Sam.

"Playboy!" said the voice from the other end of the phone.

It was Jose and Sam knew what the call was about.

"What up, homeboy," Sam said. "Did you get that on your books?" he asked.

"Yeah, I appreciate it man," Jose replied.

"It's getting crazy in here. Motherfuckers running around here in a gang raping all newbie inmates," he said.

"What?" Sam replied. "Are you good?"

"Yeah, I used some of the money on my books to recruit my own gang in here," said Jose.

Jose was always good at pulling people together thought Sam to himself. He seemed to have had some kind of inherent leadership quality about himself. Sam considered himself more as a manager because he had worked to acquire his skills at building businesses and coordinating his dreams in life into tangible goals. While Jose's ethical shortcomings had often impaired his ability, Sam didn't view the concept of a born leader as a revered position in this day and time. It was about survival of the fittest in today's world.

"But, I didn't call you about that my nigga'," he said. "Word in the streets say that them knuckle heads you had signed are talking some real hurt shit."

"Aw, them punks ain't got no heart," replied Sam.

"Exactly, they may be trying to get some," Jose stated. "I got some guys that I can send to go see those cats."

Sam was listening closely now. He knew what Jose meant and was cautious about continuing the conversation because they were on a prison line. Although Jose was behind bars, he could still reach out and call shots on the streets of Miami. He could have people come in from out of the country and have people murdered on the spot. The killers could return home and never be found for the deed they did.

"I'm good, Chico," Sam replied.

"I'm getting out the game, but I got some other things on the cooker," said Sam.

"You know I'm here and I still got your back," said Jose.

"No doubt," replied Sam. "I got a stack on your books homie, I gotta' head out."

Sam hung up the phone and pondered the conversation he just had. It felt good to know that he and Jose's relationship was strong. Friends have each other's back regardless of ethics, social status or envy. All you got is your friends; loyalty can be a binding source and a double-edged sword when it comes to friendship. The thought of going home made Sam want to binge drink. His relationship with his wife had deteriorated very badly and divorce was apparently imminent. He cut the lights in the shop and exited the premises.

***

Chapter 15: The Journey

Charlotte and Sam decided to focus on the cocaine epidemic, Cocaine Cowboy gangs and high profile rappers. They begin churning out featured cover stories and brought light to the community concerning the issues ravaging their communities. Miami's Hip Hop community was exploding with groups putting heavy baselines into their music. This began to characterize the Miami sound into rap music.

Sam's desire was to build the readership of the magazine to dominate the regional music industry of Miami and possibly establish a worldwide readership. He found in his experience in business that the grassroots approach was always a viable process. Because of his reputation in the community and his links to the music industry he began interviewing popular rap artists. The magazine readership began to increase and they were beginning to be accepted in the main stream for the profiling of the Hip Hop/Rap culture. It was now the late 1980's and Hip Hop was in full swing representing a national favor for rap music.

The members of First String were now signed to a Miami based up-and-coming rap label called Obi-Wan Kenobi records. They shortened their name and became the FS1 Crew and had experienced phenomenal hits under a new management company. The crew had become one of the top regional rap groups in Miami within only a couple of years.

Sam showed up for his meeting at Hot107 with the radio executives and was escorted by an intern to the meeting board room. The intern was a very inquisitive young man and Sam was surprised that the intern remembered him from his days as the first record label exec to do a deal with the group now known as the FS1 Crew.

"How was it working with the FS1 Crew?" the intern inquired.

"At the time they were new in the game and wet behind the ears, you know," replied Sam. "They were not real as far as being loyal to the crew and were more into being business-like instead of representing the true cause of the art."

The intern led Sam into a large spacious room where the top executives of the radio station sat around a large circular oak table. The men were discussing the music program for the yearly broadcasting plan and scarcely acknowledged Sam's entry into the room. Sam always considered them snobs, but dealt with their shallowness as consequence of his chosen career path. As the meeting progressed, Sam gave little thought to his conversation with the little known intern and continued to solicit input from local radio station concerning the state of Hip Hop in the industry.

The FS1 Crew started an all-out attack campaign against Sam and his magazine company. They slandered Sam saying he was a cheat and tried to ambush their career when he released the first album they put out. They also said that he became a journalist to attempt to sandbag their career and that he was trying to extort them for money. Sam was befuddled and didn't know how to react to the allegations. He thought his beef with the crew was old news.

Sam continued to meet with radio executives and disregarded the circus that was brewing with the FS1 allegations. He was set to meet with executives from 99Hits when he had a run-in with the president of Obi-Wan Records at the station.

"P-Man Sam, how's it going, brother," said Obi.

Obi was your classic hustler, many would say a mirror image of Sam, but he didn't think so. Although Obi was a former club owner and came up in the hood, he was a bit younger than Sam. His ethics were different and his greed for money was insatiable. Sam was from the old school of loyalty and friends. Flash and cash was the bottom line for the new generation of rap that was breaking through.

"It's all good, Obi," replied Sam. "Let me holler at you for a minute."

226

The two men stood in the parking lot of the radio station and Obi waved his entourage of lackeys to proceed on to the white on white Cadillac that awaited them. It was a well-dressed car with vogue tires and true-spoke wire wheels.

"You heated 'cause you couldn't hold your artists," Obi jabbed with his inquiry. " 'Dem boys making me paper now."

"Man, I was making paper when you were running around with your roller skates," countered Sam.

"What's up with your boys attacking me and my business?" Sam asked.

"Well, I heard you were running around telling radio Disc Jockeys that FS1 wasn't true to the art of Hip Hop and that they were in it for the loot," said Obi.

"That's not true!" replied Sam.

"Tell that to them, if you dare," Obi stated. "Lips from Hot107 said he got an exclusive from you."

Sam stood puzzled at the response he got from Obi and he was not sure if the remark was to be taken as truth. The name Lips did not ring a bell with him and he didn't have a working relationship with DJs' from radio stations. Obi strutted off in his arrogant style and paused for a minute before ducking his head inside of the car.

"Hey listen, I run a record label. Not a reunion committee." He remarked snickering as the Cadillac pulled off screeching out of the parking lot. Its vogue tires gripped the black top of the parking surface making the car spin out like a race car heading into the Miami traffic. Sam stood for a while and watched the car disappear into the throng of cars on the roadway. People had come out of the radio station among the whispers that Record President Obi-Wan was in a scuffle in the parking area. Sam ignored the stares as he proceeded to his car. He would have to disregard his current tasks and find out more about this Lips fellow.

***

Lips was a DJ that was currently the hot stuff for Hot107 and he was a former intern before he got his position. He got his break by confronting the realness of FS1 on air and questioning their commitment to making a dollar instead of being real to the music. He was the same intern that Sam spoke with on a meeting at Hot107 sometime back. That intern was Lips and he had used the information from Sam as headway into spring-boarding his career. This music industry is like a scorpion thought Sam, it will sting you every chance it gets.

Sam made his way to the Hot107 studio and waited until Lips was done completing a radio segment before confronting him.

"You Lips?" Sam asked the young man exiting the broadcast room.

"What you want?" Lips replied.

Sam snatched the kid up by his collars and shoved him against a nearby wall. Everyone in the radio station turned to watch the commotion. Local rap artist guests that were in the studio for an interview teased Lips as he struggled to get free from Sam's grasp.

"If you ever pass on grown folk business again to get your reputation, think twice," said Sam before slinging Lips like a ragdoll to the floor.

"Damn, P-Man Sam punked that nigga'," said one of the rap artist guests.

Sam exited the station quick to avoid advancing security.

***

Chapter 16: Businessman

Jose had spent two decades in prison for his crimes as a hustler in the early Cocaine Cowboy days of the Miami streets. He was released from prison and had retained some of his money from his exploits on the streets. He had maintained his criminal connections, but decided to become a business man in order to remain free. He set up a meeting with the owner of the fledgling Hot107 Radio Station and brokered a deal to purchase part ownership. As a part of the deal he would bring in some of his own Disc Jockeys, promotion and production personnel. DJ Lips was effectively dropped as a Disk Jockey at

Hot107 as Jose established himself as company executive.

Sam's old partner was back in the game so to speak and he would prove instrumental in building an empire in the music industry. Sam had not seen his friend in a couple of years and was excited to hear about his business ventures. Sam decided to pay Jose a visit at the studios of Hot107 and was in high spirits about the possibility of pitching him a business proposal.

Sam entered the spacious lobby of Hot107 and it was empty with the exception of the guard at the front desk. The guard was on the telephone as Sam entered and after a few minutes of waiting Sam took a seat in the plush leather sofa near the desk. The lobby had been newly remodeled with gold plated albums that aligned the walls. The furniture was all modern with cherry wood stained accents which gave the lobby a professional appeal.

South Florida was a diversified region with various music tastes and Hot107 was buckling under the foot of corporate majority White goliath industries. Jose had obviously become interested in the music industry due to Sam's ventures. He had used his resources to gain knowledge of the radio industry and its top managers. It was widely known throughout the media that the station was struggling, but maintained a loyal market among Black communities.

"Who are you here to see?" said the guard.

Sam was deep in thought and had not realized the guard was done with his call. He snapped up from the comfort of the sofa and proceeded towards the desk.

"I'm here for Jose Marti," stated Sam.

Just as the guard began to make the call to Jose's office he walked through the lobby. Sam walked toward him with an extended hand.

"What's happing, bro," said Sam.

"Good to see you, man," replied Jose as he pumped Sam's hand with a firm handshake.

"Let's go to my office," said Jose.

Sam was impressed with his friend's new status. He had come from the rough streets of Miami to prison and redirected his life as a business man. They walked the corridors of the radio station. The offices were designed with see-through glass walls and Sam could see the office workers scurry around with stack of papers. As they walked Jose talked of his plans to improve the radio standing in the industry. They walked to the end of the corridor which was Jose's office and entered a high ceiled room with a big oak desk near the center of the room. There was a nearby couch and a TV/VCR set in the corner of the room. A leather chair set in front of the oak desk which Sam sat on. Jose walked around the oak desk and adjusted the blinds to display a panoramic view of a nearby yacht club.

"I plan to increase the frequency watts from 16,000 to 100,000 watts. Not covering the entire Dade County area is a problem." Jose stated.

Sam was surprised to hear Jose speak in such a business manner and had speculated that Jose had accomplished a lot of study during his time in prison. Jose stood looking out of his window as he talked about his ideology for success. Jose himself was of Spanish decent, but had an undeniable tie to the Black community. Sam speculated that because Jose had perpetrated grievous acts

237

such as selling drugs and other criminal offenses he felt a certain guilt. Jose had built his street wealth on the backs of the poor and disadvantaged. Although he had served his time he now was in a position to give back by doing something positive and of substance to the community that he may have indirectly robbed.

"Well, I'm interested in getting a couple of interviews with artists that you give promotional on- air time too," said Sam.

Sam knew many new artists made visits to local radio stations to access the community in exposing their music. Sam knew if he could cultivate relationships with these new aspiring artists he could build his readership. Sam preferred his career as a magazine executive as that to the head of a rap music label. He had decided that he would do whatever it took to advance and excel in the industry.

"No problem," Jose replied.

He moved from the window and plopped down in the cushioned leather chair in front of his large desk.

"Whenever we have someone on your interested in, give me a call," he said.

Sam could see that Jose's mind was at work now. He had seen this side of him many times in some of their past business deals. Sam did not comment on Jose's response and would give him a chance to let him say what was on his mind.

"You know guys like us are often reduced to trying to start a car wash or barbershop once we get out of the life," said Jose.

Sam could see where Jose was going with the conversation and did agree on the point he foresaw him attempting to make. It was much easier to get in that kind of business rather than getting a job and going through the hassling consequences of a felony charge on your personal record.

"I realize I had a second chance when I got out of prison and I'm determined to take advantage of that," stated Jose.

There was a multitude of things from the drug game that could be learned. The business of supply and demand is easily picked up which stimulates profits. The ability to utilize a budget in all dealings and the ability to utilize math could translate into riches. Sam understood these latent principles and learned them just by observation of his friends. Jose was now in control of his destiny and would have to avoid past affiliations to keep from falling back into that life.

Chapter 17: The Climb

Sam dreamed of having a readership in the millions for the magazine company and considered various options for selling shares in the business. He attended various societal networking functions around Miami and West Palm Beach. Sam also coordinated fund raisers at the Historical Black Institutions of Miami. This endeavor was fertile ground in cultivating friendly relations with the youth that were entrenched in the Hip Hop culture. Sam committed himself to peddling shares to anyone he thought would have an interest in buying them.

Publishing the magazine was done on a monthly basis which demanded a strict adherence to scheduling. Sam worked to increase circulation by utilizing U.S. radio and movie theaters throughout the region. He developed advertising skits with the assistance of local rap artists and worked with DJ's to promote during radio shows. He utilized the street team concept in handing out flyers to movie goers in theater parking lots. Sam was managing street team efforts at a local movie theater when he was approached by a patron.

"Hey, you're P-Man Sam," said a young lady with braids in her hair.

"Yeah, I'm him. Take a flyer," Sam replied.

He handed the girl a couple of copies of the flyer being distributed. The parking lot was busy with people heading to the next movie showing. Sam posted people at the front entrance giving away flyers and free copies of old magazine issues. The girl seemed intrigued by the flyer as she looked it over and she then put it into her pocket.

"You know there was a rumor you got DJ Lips fired?" she stated.

Sam, with a puzzled look on his face, began to stammer and could not immediately understand what the girl was implying. She looked at him suspiciously awaiting his response. She was a young brown-skinned beauty with long curly black hair and as she waited for his response she popped the gum she was chewing with her mouth.

"Miss, I don't recall a DJ Lips," Sam replied.

The girl gave a look as not to understand Sam's response. She blew a bubble and smacked her lips as she chewed the gum.

"He used to have a show at Hot107," the girl chirped.

Sam knew that Jose had taken on an ownership role at Hot107 and now fully realized what the girl was implying. Jose must have replaced staff at the station upon his role as an executive at the company and replaced personnel with his people. Jose had not mentioned firing anyone to him and why would he? Sam reasoned to himself. Jose as part owner had no obligation to Sam outside of their relations as friends. Additionally, Sam was unaware that Jose knew what had transpired with the whole DJ Lips scenario.

"I know nothing about that," Sam replied.

In the industry there are a lot of incidences where people place blame on other parties for their misfortunes. Sam did not care much about what had happened to Lips and certainly would not lose sleep over it. He was now swimming with sharks and had to adapt in order to progress as a good business man. He had put the Lips incident behind him and was preoccupied with other relevant things in his life. He had the possibility of divorce brewing with his wife, an incident brewing with his former label artists and pressure building in his magazine business. As Sam pondered this revelation the girl walked away shaking her head.

"I knew it," she muttered under her breath.

***

Sam's efforts in selling stock in the business were bearing fruit and he had raised around $100,000 from wealthy supporters in the city. Dividend income was beginning to trickle in and the company seemed to be prospering. Sam felt empowered in seeing his efforts produce tangible benefits for the company. As he entered the office for the morning to perform some business calls and paperwork he encountered Charlotte at the front entrance.

"I'm really worried about your old affiliations with that rap group First String," she said.

"Why is that an issue," Sam responded.

Sam held the door as the two walked into the office building. He could smell the light scent of coffee brewing and it made him hunger for a cup of Joe. He loved the smell of coffee in the morning and it gave him a sense of relief despite what hectic occurrences were amidst.

"I have a source in with one of our local competitors that they plan to boycott us," she said.

"That's ridiculous," responded Sam.

He was unsure why the group members were targeting him for such a move. He assumed because of his growing influence in the industry that it was just a publicity plow for media attention. He had been nothing but professional and fair to those guys he reasoned to himself.

"Listen, don't worry about it. Those guys are just angling for media," Sam stated.

Charlotte still appeared concerned about the issue. As the original founding member of the business she had invested a great deal of time and money into establishing the organization. She did not want to lose everything for which they had worked. Economically they could ill afford financial sanctions that could develop as a result of being black listed. Sam knew he had to take extra measures to reassure Charlotte.

"Listen, I met with Jose and we have discussed aligning interests to capture the southeast regional market in advertising. Let's focus on solidifying those negotiations and then we can deal with these circulating rumors." Sam said.

Charlotte seemed very delighted at the possibility of working with Hot107 and knew that Sam had great relations with Jose. Sam could see that she was more at ease after hearing his plans and further assured her by noting the accessibility they would have to reaching the masses throughout the airwaves of Miami. Sam didn't think the group members had the juice or organization to wage such a plan. He was certain his alliance with Hot107 would be a great counter if they did try to boycott their magazine.

***

Jose knew he would need to be an innovative leader in taking on an ownership role and he could use his friend Sam to make a mark in sales for the company. He would sell air-time to Sam in the 7pm-midnight slot to reach late night listeners that are partying and not tied to work or school. This would be a discounted rate for Sam because it was not prime time air. It would help sales in capturing new listeners tied to the growing Hip Hop culture which could boost the stations profile among the youth. Jose also knew he could promote his business with the use of Sam's magazine which would capture some of the paper's readership.

Miami's only Black station Hot107 was said to have been the lowest in the rankings of the regional market. With the help of Sam's links to the music industry and the print magazine world, the outmoded ways of the station could be revamped. The Urban

Contemporary format would be the design plan that Jose knew would be the future.

Sam previously made Jose aware of a possible boycott of Bandstand Magazine and Jose knew it was in the best interest of the radio station to offer support. Jose decided to stand against other media groups that supported any sort of boycott of the magazine. As rumors swirled on the streets many prepared for the fallout that could possibly result from the storm.

Chapter 18: Seal

Members of the First String Rap Crew boycotted the magazine. Their current record label Obi-Wan Kenobi records supported their efforts by buying out the magazine cover of a rival magazine company. Any ad placed with Sam's company was pulled pending further notice. The group released a dis record about Sam and other organizations affiliated with his magazine entity. The group tried to get on-air interview time with Hot107 to promote the boycott not knowing the station was aligned with Sam's cause. Sam was no punk and he fired back with fierce editorials condemning the actions of First String. Sam printed a cover on his magazine with him holding the severed heads of all the First String members and him standing on the prone body of the their record label president Obi-Wan. Jose contributed to the fight by promoting the cover edition on radio blasts throughout the city.

"Did you run the broadcast on the story I printed this month?" Sam asked as he stood in Jose's office.

"Sure did bro and its boosting my listenership," replied Jose.

He took a Black and Mild from his humidor; holding it with his thumb and pinky he lit it. He reared back in his gator skin chair rolling it between his fingers. Jose took a long drag before he offered it to Sam.

"Let's celebrate, they got no fight for us," said Jose.

"I'll celebrate when this thing is over," Sam replied shirking away from the cigar.

"Man, we got those fools by their short and curlies," Jose continued.

Sam was not content with what was being said on the streets. He wanted victories by way of the courts and through the media. A street cred victory meant little to him at this point and he wanted to prove he was a professional legit businessman. As Sam departed Jose's office at the station, he decided to prepare for the upcoming court battles by conferencing with his attorney while relaxing at home. The next coming week would be a big one as they were due in court for a final

showdown on the issue.

***

First String attempted to sue for

defamation and copyright infringement. The

federal courts allowed an injunction to limit

distribution of Sam's magazine edition. Sam

ignored the order and printed mass copies

claiming freedom of the press rights. Sam

eventually got the lawsuits dismissed against

his organization and without notice First String

withdrew its lawsuit.

"Man, what a lovely day," said Sam to

Jose as they stood outside the federal court

house of downtown Miami.

"Now can we celebrate?" inquired Jose

as a huge smile crept across his face.

"Now we can party!" exclaimed Sam.

"Let's meet up at my office," stated Jose.

"I'll have the interns set out a platter of food

and I always keep drinks in my bar."

"Ok, cool." Sam replied.

Sam got in his car and pulled onto I-95

headed towards the radio station. He

increased the speed of his car as the traffic

moved especially fast during certain times of

the day. He lowered his windows as it seemed

a beautiful day. He also felt good about

winning his court case and the outside breeze

was cool. As Sam was driving on the interstate

he was cut off as he attempted to change lanes

to get off at his exit. He missed the exit and blew his horn at the black car that caused him to miss the exit. The car pulled up to the passenger side of his car matching his speed and the driver held up a middle finger at him. The driver looked familiar to Sam and he suddenly realized he was looking at Lips. As soon as he came to that realization he could hear a volley of gunfire. Sam's arms and legs seemed as if they were on fire and he wanted to get away from the pain. He jerked the steering wheel by reaction trying to avoid the direction the pain was emanating from and hit the concrete median. Sam's car crumpled like a piece of scrap paper as it waned to a screeching halt on the roadway. Some cars behind and around Sam braked as his scrubbed the median coming to a stop. The black car jetted forward down the roadway corridor. Sam could feel the life gushing from his body as he laid his head back against the headrest of the car seat.

His chest heaved up and down; the breath went in and out as he coughed up thick gobs of blood. He thought of his wife, he thought about his business, he thought about his family, he thought about having kids, he thought about Charlotte, he thought about the members of First String, he thought about Jose and he thought about Lips. He could hear sirens in the distance and the smell of twisted metal was pungent.

"I had plans to accomplish so much," said Sam. He expired as the sound of sirens neared his mangled vehicle.

***

Thank you for reading; Notorious P-Man Sam; check out other titles from Thomas Barr Jr. and more at Printhousebooks.com

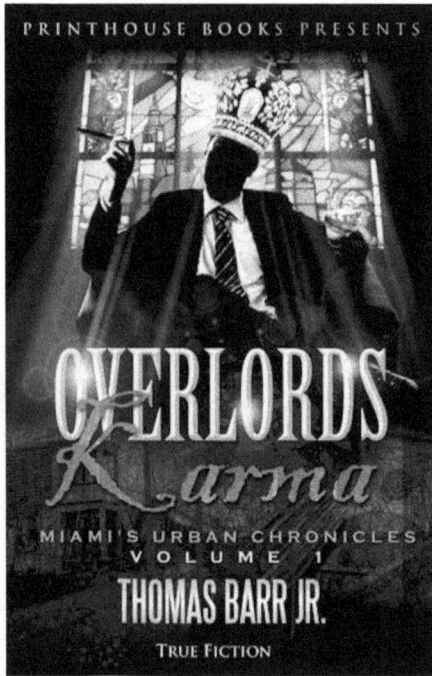

A policeman remembered the day of the
death of Miami commissioner Amp Tate.
Blood oozed over the marble floor of the most
prominent news institution in Miami.
Powerful commissioner Anthony "Amp" Tate

laid stretched out with a gaping hole in his chest. With the gun still clutched in his hand, he attempted to speak to those gathered around him as he gasped his final breaths and died. Days before, Tate was indicted on corruption charges and profiled in Miami News as the City of Miami's most corrupt politician.

Tate, a towering 6 foot -5 inch tall African American, was the commissioner of the only black district in Miami. He previously held the position as chair of the commission and was current head of the Overtown Development Corporation, with additional duties of entertainment permitting. Tate a self-made man represented the interests and concerns of Miami's black community.

The policeman stationed in the lobby of the Miami News building rushed over when he heard the shot and screams. An elderly woman with her hands filled with a stack of papers fainted and littered the floor with her correspondences. The papers were soon matted with the commissioner's bright red blood as it leaked over the floor of the lobby. The cop stood over the commissioner uncertain what to do, as he had seen many fatal gunshot wounds of this sort.

This man has bought it, he thought to himself. People scattered sprinting for the lobby stairway and exit doors. He yelled for someone to call 9-1-1. The cop jumped back from the body being careful not to get blood on his shiny black boots. Blood spewed from the hole in the commissioner's back as the bullet had ripped clean thru his chest. The cop looked on in pity as the commissioner's body initiated a series of involuntary jerks from his stiffened limbs.

Two men initially in line ahead of the commissioner peered over the officer's shoulder at the body. "I wonder what he was trying to say," said one man looking down on the corpse.

PRINTHOUSE BOOKS
Read it, Enjoy it, Tell a friend.

VIP INK Publishing Group, Incorporated.
Atlanta, GA.

www.PrintHouseBooks.com